Your World, Better

Global Progress
And
What You Can Do About It

Charles Kenny

Contents

Introduction: On the Up

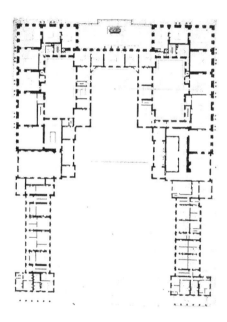

Plan of the first floor of King Louis XIV's Versailles: Spot the Bathroom (Source: Wikimedia)

Jean Nocret's painting of the family of Louis XIV. The King is the one with the scepter, his wife Queen Maria Theresa is at his elbow. Straight below the king is Louis jr. who died age 50; the portrait of the two girls at the bottom is of Anne and Marie, both of whom died aged about one month; at Louis jr.s' feet is Marie Therese, (died age five); next to the peacock is Philippe Charles (died age three). After this painting. Louis XIV had one more child, Louis François, who died at five months.

Louis XIV (the Fourteenth) reigned over France for 72 years, from 1643 to 1715. Calling himself 'The Sun King,' he ruled with absolute authority over the most powerful country in Europe. As symbol of his dominance, he built the immense Palace of Versailles, home to more than 350 people and regular host to 6,000 courtiers. Its famed Hall of Mirrors was lit by 3,000 candles. The gardens had a zoo, 400 sculptures and more than a thousand fountains.

But for all his wealth and power, Louis' life was filled with tragedy. He and his wife Maria Theresa had six children but only one survived into adulthood. Three kids died as infants, Philippe Charles died at three of a chest infection and Marie Therese at age five from tuberculosis —a bacterial disease that eats away your lungs. Even their longest-lived child, Louis the Grand Dauphin, did not survive long enough to become king after his father, dying of smallpox at the age of fifty. The Sun King's wife Maria died at 44, from infection. And he himself died at age 77 when his leg was infected with gangrene, which rots flesh.

Beyond good health, King Louis's family lacked a lot else: their palace may have had a thousand fountains, but it didn't have a single flush toilet – lucky people went in a bowl that servants would remove, others just squatted in a corner. And while six thousand candles may sound like a lot, they produce about the same amount of illumination as a couple of modern light bulbs. Most of Versailles would have been pitch black as soon as it got dark.

When it comes to quality of life, you may have it better than the family of the Sun King. You definitely have it better when it comes to remaining alive: it is doubtful that any of his family would have died as they did if they'd had access to modern medicine. And this was the wealthiest family in the most sumptuous house in the land –the vast majority of French people at the time lived lives that we would simply find unbearable. The world is just a much better place to inhabit than it was 300 years ago. But it is also a much better place to live in than it was 30 years ago. And that is the first thing that this book is about: how the life on the planet is improving.

One way of looking at that improvement is to think about the chance you'd be reading this book if I'd written it a few hundred years ago. There is a very good probability you would have been too dead to read it. Even if alive, the likelihood you could read *anything* was small: literacy was a rare skill. Books were incredibly expensive, and most people were very poor, so even if you were in the tiny minority both literate and alive you probably wouldn't have been able to afford a copy. And in many times and places this book would have been banned –it speaks approvingly of things that were often illegal or at least very dangerous to suggest, from freedom to believe in the god of your choice (or none at all) through gay rights to democracy.

Young (and old) people are getting sick less often, fewer people never learn to read or write, not as many are getting arrested by the police because of what they think and believe, less are getting hit or shot, and a lot less people are being told it's the law that the color of your skin or your gender makes you a worse person.

It might come as a surprise that the world is getting better. Most people believe poverty is getting worse worldwide and that most other people are miserable. Ask someone your grandparents' age if things have improved since they were young and they might well say no. Only about one out of every three older people in the United States think life is better today than it was fifty years ago —and these are the people who are old enough to remember fifty years ago.

But even after Covid-19, even despite the tragedies of the past few years, I think they are wrong.

Mostly, people remember the good stuff and forget the bad stuff about their past. Adults tend to remember childhood as a time of boundless energy where there was nothing to worry about and a lot of fun to be had. Life as a kid is more complicated than that. But its why older people can say "you don't know how lucky you are" and "things were better in my day" pretty much straight after each other. They mean "you are lucky to be young but unlucky to be a kid today rather than when I was a kid." I'd say the truth is closer to the other way around —although there *are* some really good bits about being young.

Ask someone in their seventies or eighties what they got sick with, and what their friends got sick with. Or ask them about "duck and cover" drills at school, when they practiced for war with Russia and the atomic bombs that would fall. Or ask them about how African Americans were treated in restaurants, on trains, or in the school system.

Or ask someone your parents' age about where they could watch a show –just one TV in the house, maybe, which had maybe four or five things to watch. Ask them if they wore a seatbelt in the back of the car. Ask them about 'acid rain.' Their answers might be reason for them –and you– to think hard about the good old days, and how good they were compared to now.

And even though life in America has got better since your parents or your grandparents were young, life in the rest of the world has got better even faster. We are really fortunate we live in this country, because people in the U.S. are still amongst the healthiest, the most educated, and the richest worldwide. But the rest of the planet is catching up. From Asia to Africa to South America, fewer people are dying young, fewer people don't learn to read, fewer people urinate or defecate in a field or street rather than in a toilet.

In the past years of pandemic, economic crisis and mass unemployment, the violent death of innocent people and violence aimed at those who protest those deaths, war, hurricanes, corruption and abuse, certainly the world *hasn't* gotten better for many of us. A lot of bad stuff still happens. And some things are getting worse. That's the second thing this book is about.

Some people still die young. Many people lose a parent or a grandparent –or more than one—way too early. Families still live lives of hunger and misery. Covid-19 and its impacts demonstrate we can backtrack on health and poverty. People still get locked up, often for things that shouldn't be a crime. Racism, sexism, and abuse of minorities remains rampant worldwide. Amongst the things that are getting worse, progress towards democracy has reversed in recent years, the coral reefs are bleaching, and the climate is getting hotter.

Perhaps it is not enough to know there's less bad stuff happening when so much bad stuff is still happening. Certainly, in a world richer and more technologically advanced than ever, it is more shocking than ever that some people remain living in extreme deprivation. But past progress does suggest that there's nothing inevitable about tragedy or misery. If we work together, the world can continue to improve. That's the third thing this book is about: what you can do to help make sure things keep on getting better and to reverse the trends pointing in the wrong direction.

No individual human being has solved a global problem by themselves, but billions have been part of solutions. And you can be, too.

We are talking about change on a large scale – this book is about a whole planet. Think about all of the people you know –not just friends or family, just anyone you've met and remember. Most people know somewhere between 300 and 600 people. A small town, or a medium-size sports arena, holds about thirty times the number of people you know –around 15,000. A big city like New York has about nine million people in it. That's 600 stadiums –or about 18,000 times the number of people you know.

There are about seven billion, five hundred and thirty million —or 7,530,000,000— people on the planet. That is more than 800 New York cities, or 500,000 stadiums, or about 15 million times the number of people you know. If you tried to meet all the humans on Earth, spending every hour of every day of an eighty-year life meeting new people, you'd have long enough to say a very quick 'hi' to each one —about a third of a second.

All those people you'll never meet have hopes and fears, friends and family, things to do and things they want to do. It matters if you get sick or are attacked and it matters the same for all seven billion, five hundred and twenty-nine million, nine hundred and ninety-nine thousand nine hundred and ninety-nine other people on the planet.

But it is hard to think about big numbers of people as *people*, not just a statistic: we are better at understanding and engaging with stories about one person than lots of them. Tragedies in movies focus on the suffering of a few people, not armies of them. Hundreds of extras get shot without a second thought while the star gets slow motion and a long final close-up as they grimace through their last lines. Similarly, in real life it is hard to picture ten thousand people having a bad day and really feel the same sorrow as we do when our friend has a rotten time –let alone feel ten thousand times the sorrow. It is too overwhelming. But it is important to understand that there *are* people behind the numbers.

And if the scale of global sadness can seem overwhelming, it is easy to forget the scale of happiness is usually even bigger. Imagine our stadium full of people having a great time at a concert. Those fifteen thousand people feeling happy is pretty good. Ten million would be even better. A billion would be fantastic.

Every hour across the world, 15,000 kids – enough to fill the stadium– are born. That's four each second, and it generates a lot of happy parents, grandparents, sisters, and brothers. Every day, about twenty million people celebrate a birthday. In the US alone, about six thousand people get married each 24 hours, and many more than that make a new friend. About 50 million kids graduate high school worldwide each year. In the US, on the average day when there isn't a pandemic, 3,600,000 people go to the cinema to watch a movie. More than that dance or sing or laugh –or at least smile. Billions worldwide see someone they like or learn something new.

There are an immense amount of people doing pretty well in life, all things considered. If you ask Americans "is life exciting, routine or dull," more than half say "exciting." Or ask people across the planet how many had moments of happiness, laughter, and enjoyment the day before, it comes to about 5.6 billion people –about three quarters of Earth's population. A little less than a third of all people felt worry, sadness, or anger at some point during that day –again, the world isn't anywhere near perfect. But it is mostly filled with people having more good times than bad, and fewer bad times than the generation before them. It's a start, and we –you– can build on it.

In the following chapters I am going to talk about how America and the World has changed over the past few decades –what has happened to people's health, their wealth, their homes and at school, how happy they feel and how they spend their free time. We'll discuss war and violence, political freedoms and rights and the environment. In every chapter we will look at the things that have gotten better, the problems and challenges that remain, and what you can help do about them. I hope you'll finish the book a little more optimistic about the state of the planet and a little more committed to make it better still.

(One more thing: I'm going to imagine your grandparents were born about seventy-five years ago, and your parents about forty-five years ago. That's a bit before most parents and grandparents of middle school students in the United States, but it is a bit younger than my kids' parents (me) and their grandparents. So, when I talk about 'when they were young' I mean the 1980s for your parents and the 1950s for your grandparents, and 'when they were born' the 1970s for parents and 1940s for grandparents.)

14

Health

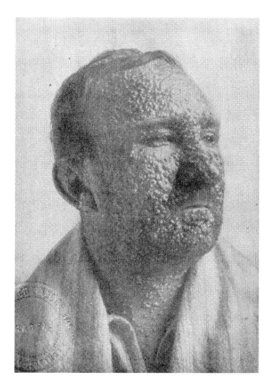

A smallpox victim from Illinois in 1912.
Thankfully, smallpox has been eradicated worldwide.
(Source: Wikimedia)

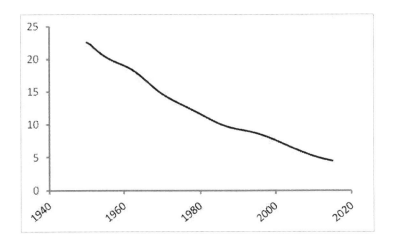

*The percentage of children born worldwide over the last 70 years who
died before their fifth birthday.*

If you grew up watching Disney movies, you might think the most dangerous thing to be in history was a parent. Belle has a dad but no mom, Aladdin is an orphan and Jasmine has lost her mother, the Frozen sisters' parents sink to the bottom of the sea soon after the opening credits. But in fact, being a child was *far* more dangerous than being an adult for most of history. We saw in the introduction that all of King Louis and Queen Maria's kids died before the king himself did. That's hardly the only example. And the immense risks of the early days of life are a reason that a lot of traditions around celebrating a birth and naming children wait until a week or more after the child is born —from christening (in Christianity) through brita and bris (Judaism) to Aqiqah (Islam) and Namkaran (Hinduism).

Worldwide, your first day is still the day of life you have most chance of dying on, and the first week of life the most dangerous week, with the first year the most dangerous year. Congratulations on making it through. But you face a lot lower chance of dying as a child than did your ancestors, or even your grandparents. In 1950 in the US, more than one in twenty-five children born didn't live to their 15th birthday —about one for each classroom of kids. Today less than one in every 125 children in the US die before the age of fifteen.

A major reason for that is the decline of childhood diseases. Take measles —the symptoms are a high fever, runny nose, a bad cough, and a red rash all over your body for a week or more. It used to be a dangerous condition, leading to more serious illnesses and sometimes death. And the coughs and sneezes are incredibly infectious, much more so even than Covid-19. If someone with measles sneezes near you and you don't have any protection against the virus, there's a very good chance you'll catch it. When your grandparents were kids, if they didn't get measles, they probably had friends who did. Half a million children a year got measles in the US in the 1950s.

A vaccine was developed against measles in the 1960s. And, since then, the disease has become extremely rare. It is amongst a number of infections that used to be common in the US that have been wiped out or close to it thanks to vaccines and other medical advances. Other illnesses you won't get include yellow fever (symptoms from muscle aches to organ failure), smallpox (body-wide blisters, diarrhea, death), malaria (sweating, fever, convulsions, coma), polio (vomiting, pain, paralysis), diphtheria (sore throat, difficulty breathing) and roundworm (bloody spit, asthma, muscle pains).

And when it comes to medical advances for adults, todays older people are taking a lot of medicines that were invented since they were children. Here are the top five most common medicines prescribed by a doctor in the US: Lisinopril helps reduce blood pressure, which helps prevent heart attacks or strokes (where a blood vessel in the brain gets blocked or bursts). It started being used in the US in 1987. Atorvastatin and Simvastatin both help lower cholesterol, a fatty substance also linked to heart attacks and strokes. Atorvastatin started being prescribed in the US in 1996 and Simvastatin in 1992. Metformin helps people with diabetes. It started being used in the United States in 1995. Levothyroxine treats hypothyroidism –a disease that can cause tiredness and depression—and it is the only medicine amongst the top five that was already around when your parents were young.

If someone your grandparents' or parents' age had high blood pressure or high cholesterol or diabetes before these medicines were invented, they'd probably be sicker, and maybe even dead. I'm one of them. I also have a couple of stents, a technology developed in 1977. These metal tubes are in a vein that keeps blood flowing to my heart, so my heart can keep blood flowing everywhere else. I'm very grateful to medical progress for the fact that I'm healthy.

Taking a drive has changed a lot over time as well. When your grandparents were kids, lots of cars didn't have seatbelts –a law saying new cars had to have them was only passed in 1968. When your parents were young, lots of people still didn't *use* seatbelts: New York was the first state to say you had to wear one, in 1984. Children would sit unrestrained in the front of the car, the back of the car, the trunk—and climb back and forth between them as they shot along a highway at speeds that are now illegal. In a crash, all too often they'd simply cannon through the front window to land head-first on the road. New rules and regulations about how cars are built and how you can drive and ride in them are a big reason why the risk of dying in a traffic accident in America is about one sixth what it was in the 1950s and 1960s.

Cars aren't the only things that have got considerably safer in America: your chance of being killed by a lightning strike was 37 times higher in 1900 than it is today. The chances a person will die from fall off a high building or a cliff is down by nearly three quarters and we've seen similar drops in the risk of dying in a fire or drowning. Thanks to staying inside or near tall buildings with lightning conductors during storms, firefighters, lifeguards, railings, flotation devices, swimming lessons and laws and regulations about safety, being alive in America is just a lot less dangerous than it used to be.

More good news is that the rest of the world is catching up. Worldwide, fewer people are getting sick and dying young while more people are living long, healthy lives.

Centuries ago, in most places, the average newborn could expect to live for less than thirty years. About two out of every five babies born did not live to see their fifth birthday. In some countries and in bad times, more than half of all kids died by the age of five. Families back then were larger, too —with four or five kids the usual. That meant most parents had to bury a child. It was an expected part of being a mother or father. And most people had at least one brother or sister who died when they were young. Thankfully, today, and worldwide, parents burying their children is an increasingly rare tragedy.

In the decade your grandparents were born, someone born in Africa could expect to live just to 37 years old —probably younger than your parents are. Today that's up to 62 years old, closer to the age of your grandparents. That's still too short —a child born in the United States can expect to live to 79 years old. Those extra seventeen years are thanks to better food and healthcare and a safer environment. But the good news is that it isn't too late for today's kids in Africa to get the opportunity for an even longer life —if the region keeps on getting richer, healthier, and better fed, then the gap will shrink further.

Just since 1990, 100 million children's lives have been saved from reduced death rates from infectious diseases like measles and malaria –that's about the same as the total population of California, Texas, New York State and Pennsylvania combined. That is largely thanks to health measures including bed nets (to keep malaria-infected mosquitoes away) and vaccinations. Four in five children worldwide have been vaccinated against measles, for example.

(Children haven't only been the biggest winners from vaccination, they were vital to some of the research that went into developing them. When Dr Edward Jenner wanted to test his theory that getting a case of the irritating but undeadly cowpox protected you against mass murdering smallpox, he needed a test subject who he could be confident hadn't had the disease already. Jenner turned to James Phipps, the eight-year-old son of his gardener, who had not yet been exposed. Taking a needle, he drew out pus from the cowpox blister of a local milkmaid and then rubbed it into two small cuts in James' arm. The boy got a minor case of the chills, and then felt fine. But a few weeks later, to see if James was immune, Dr Jenner stabbed him with a needle dipped in smallpox pus. And then did it again, nineteen more times. Luckily, Jenner's theory was right, otherwise James could have done worse than simply feeling like a pin cushion –he could have died or at least got seriously sick. The doctor got worldwide fame and considerable fortune from the experiment; James had to be satisfied with Jenner's present of a house to live in rent-free).

Beyond vaccines, we'll see there has been a considerable global spread of water and sewer networks. And a global infrastructure to deliver food means ever fewer people have too little to eat. When your grandparents were young, millions of people starved to death in the average year. When your parents were young, famine was still in the news all the time, including massive famines in Cambodia and Ethiopia. Thankfully, large-scale famines are almost completely a thing of the past, with death rates a small fraction of the 1960s. Most years, some countries still see their crops fail. But thanks to earlier detection of poor harvests and a network of international agencies that can ship stuff to people who might need food or the money to buy it, that rarely results in people starving. Again, the proportion of kids worldwide under the age of five that are very low weight because of inadequate food fell from one quarter to less than one seventh between 1990 and 2017.

There are still many millions of people with serious health problems in the United States and even more in the rest of the world. Getting richer is only limited protection against dying from cancer, for example, and more than one out of twenty people in the US have the illness. Death rates from cancer as well as heart disease are slowly declining as people stop smoking and treatment improves, but it is still a major killer.

Again, a lot of American adults have become addicted to painkilling drugs. We'll discuss in a later chapter the fact that too many people remain depressed. Even more American adults –about four out of every ten—are obese. That can increase people's risk of strokes, heart disease and diabetes. And about 27 million people in the United States don't have easy access to good care from doctors and nurses because they don't have health insurance, which costs around $10,000 a year to buy.

Globally, about two in five adults worldwide are overweight or obese, up from one in five adults when your parents were young. Linked to that is the fact that about forty percent of the world's adults have high blood pressure. More of those who don't die young from infections are dying older from illnesses including strokes, heart attacks and cancer.

And still, one in every twenty-five babies born worldwide won't live to the age of five. Even though that's down from about one out of seven when your parents were young, or one out of five when your grandparents were children, it's still a huge tragedy. It adds up to more than five million kids a year.

About 1.9 million children die each year in their first month of life. For those who survive that month, about 649 children under the age of five die worldwide each year in natural disasters like earthquakes and floods. About 49,000 are killed in road accidents. But the biggest killers are still infectious diseases: 83,000 die from measles and 86,000 from whooping cough. Malaria kills

354,000, diarrhea 534,000 and pneumonia and other respiratory diseases 809,000.

And for all the spread of obesity, more than 800 million people worldwide are still under-nourished –they don't get enough food energy to be healthy and active. When kids don't get enough food, they don't grow as tall, a phenomenon called stunting. In Kenya, a country in East Africa, about a quarter of five-year-olds are stunted because of malnutrition.

The good news is that most of these deaths and illnesses are preventable. To help deal with the obesity epidemic in the US, provide easy access to exercise and encourage walking, ensure everyone has access to good food, and control the ways that high-sugar and high fat foods are sold and advertised (they may be 'Grrreat!', but one cup of Frosties has eleven ounces of sugar). School meals could be both healthy and tasty, even if it might cost a little more than the current average of $2 a day to make them. Health care is also a problem of money, one that every other rich country in the World apart from the United States solves by paying for the health system using taxes rather than asking people to buy insurance. Many poorer countries have introduced this 'universal' health care too, even if it doesn't cover more expensive treatments.

We could make further massive progress in reducing child deaths worldwide with a few simple techniques. Make sure every baby gets vaccinated. If they live in tropical climates with lots of mosquitoes, ensure everyone sleeps under a net. Make sure everyone worldwide has enough money to buy good food, and they have somewhere to go to the toilet where their waste won't end up in drinking water or the food chain. Ensure there's a clinic nearby stocked with medicines, and that parents know what to do if their kids get diarrhea (sugar and salt mixed in water saves lives). Make sure girls in particular go to school –because educated mothers help keep children alive. None of this is particularly expensive or hard, but all too often it still doesn't happen.

And the recent past has demonstrated that for all the benefits of a globally connected planet, it increases the risk that new diseases can travel worldwide at the speed of flight. Covid-19 reversed recent progress against death: in 2020, it brought us about back to the global death rate of a decade ago. If the world had been better prepared with testing and tracing systems to find those who had been exposed to the virus, if people had worn masks, stayed distant and (when they could) stayed home, fewer people would have died.

On the other hand, for most of history closing schools and businesses as an effort to slow the spread of the disease would have been largely pointless: sparing hospital capacity would have made little difference because hospitals had so few effective tools to save lives. And holding down caseloads in the hope of a vaccine or cure would have been hoping in vain. We smashed all previous records in taking less than a year between the emergence of Covid-19 and the development of the first vaccines. Our progress has made this global tragedy less tragic than it would have been.

One of the best things *you* can do for the health of people in your community is stay healthy yourself. If you don't have a cold, the flu or measles, you can't give it to someone else. So, wash hands, eat well and get enough sleep. And make sure you are vaccinated. If you can't *get* measles or Covid-19, nor can you *give* it to anyone. It is particularly important that everyone who can get vaccinated does get vaccinated because people with weak immune systems can't. They rely on the rest of us not getting sick to stop them from getting sick.

Staying healthy is one of those things that when you do something good for you, you are also doing something good for other people too. And that is a big part of global progress. Economists call this a 'spillover benefit' and one of the biggest ever involves smallpox. You didn't get vaccinated against smallpox when you were young –despite that smallpox can kill and there is a vaccine. The reason is that the world's countries working together wiped it out around the time when your parents were born. Last century, 100 million people died from the disease. This century, no-one should. Because enough people got vaccinated to protect themselves fifty years ago, future generation get the spillover benefit of smallpox being wiped out.

A recent incident at Disneyland in California demonstrates what happens when vaccination doesn't –and economists call that a 'negative spillover'. Every month, about two million people go to the park. Before Christmas in 2014, one of those millions had measles. Fifty-four other people who went to Disneyland were infected. They went home to states including Arizona and Colorado and countries including Mexico and Canada. They got sick, and went on to give measles to more people. Most of those who got sick at Disneyland hadn't been fully vaccinated. It ruined their new year *and* endangered other people. In the last year we've seen a lot of negative spillovers related to Covid-19 – don't wear a mask, or don't stay six feet from people, and you are more likely to infect them if you are sick.

There is also a spillover benefit from being calm in the car while someone is driving –and a negative one from shouting. Again, making sure that the driver is concentrating rather than texting or calling doesn't just make your journey safer, it makes it safer for everyone else on the road with you. Think of it as a vaccine for car safety.

If you want to help people the world over towards better health, there are some organizations you can support that work to provide basic health care for all. UNICEF, the United Nations Fund for

Children, provides vaccines along with other health care and nutrition to kids who need it worldwide. Deworm the World provides drugs to schoolchildren that kills a small worm egg that can be eaten with infected food. After the egg hatches, the worm takes up residence in the intestine where it sucks away nutrients and releases more eggs. The pills only cost cents but reliably wipe out the parasites. The Against Malaria Foundation provides bed nets to keep out mosquitoes to families living in places where lots of people get malaria. You can also write to your representatives in Congress to ask them to support health care for all here in the US and abroad.

However long you can expect to live, everyone still dies in the end. When a person dies after a long life. those left behind feel the void. But at least they have lived for many, hopefully mostly happy, years. The more people who do that, the better. And that is what's happening –everywhere.

Money

The Kaburas in front of their house in the province of Makamba in Burundi. The family lives on less than $4 a day —for everything. Source: Gapminder/Dollar Street

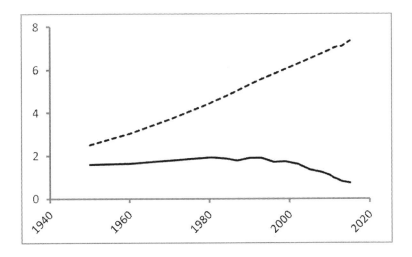

*The World population (in billions) living on less than $1.90 a day
(solid line) and total (dotted line)*

For most of history most people hardly ever used money. They ate what they grew on their farmland and often paid rent or tithes to church and lord in the form of crops or farm animals. They made their own shelter and furniture and swapped things they'd made for things they needed. Money was something rich people used, and it was usually made from expensive metals –silver and gold. Today, most people use money every day and mostly it isn't made from anything at all: it is just numbers recorded in computers. We pay for things over the Internet and phone from shops next door and people around the world. We couldn't use coins to do that even if there was much more gold and silver around.

One reason for the change: a lot more people have a lot more money than they used to –they are richer. In 1500, the world produced $430,000,000,000 worth of goods and services each year –from food to entertainment. Today, the world produces $108,000,000,000,000 in stuff and services –or about two hundred and fifty times as much. That value of dollar bills would pile up to thirty stacks each stretching to the moon. There are more people around today than in 1500 –maybe fifteen times as many—but the average person is still a LOT better off. They are seventeen times richer, give or take.

Global economic growth has never been as fast as it has been over the past century. Even in the US, if you were to ask your parents if you had more stuffed animals, books, art supplies and games growing up than they had, the answer would likely come back a resounding 'yes!' You probably eat out and order in lots more than they did as well –the average person nowadays does it about four times a week. One reason: most American families have more money than when your parents lived with your grandparents.

When your grandparents were young, the average American spent about $27 a day on things from food through housing and cinema tickets to healthcare, holidays, and cars –that's for each child and adult. By the time your parents were young, that had climbed to about $44 a day for each person. Today, the average person in America spends about $110 each day.

(Just to note: things were cheaper when your grandparents were young, but the numbers in this book account for changing costs, so what the average American spent when your grandparents were young would buy you as much as $27 would buy you today. That's called 'inflation adjusting,' and all the dollar numbers in this book have been inflation adjusted.)

And, worldwide, people can afford to buy considerably more now than their grandparents could. Back when your grandparents were young, the average person in the world had $9 to live on each day. By the time your parents were young that was $16. Today it is closer to $40. The world as a whole sees an average income about as high as the United States when your grandparents were born, and it is slowly catching up to the level of the United States today.

As the world has become richer, the number of people living in the most desperate poverty worldwide has been declining. One measure of global extreme poverty is based on what governments in some of the world's poorest countries say counts as being poor in those countries. Most of the richest people in those places consume amounts that would be considered poverty in the United States. Less than one in two hundred families in the East African country of Burundi live above the poverty line set by the US government for American families, for example. So, what is considered 'being poor' in Burundi is *really* poor. The global extreme poverty level using measures from countries like Burundi suggests a person is poor if they have $1.90 a day or less to spend on everything each day. Arcade and Jeannine Kabura and their children, pictured at the start of the chapter, live on even less than that.

In the US, $1.90 is enough to pay for ten to twenty minutes of babysitting, or fries at McDonalds. The average American family spends about $2 a person a day on clothes, and an average of $3 per person per day on eating out. So families living on $1.90 a person a day are spending less on *everything* than the average American family spends just on clothes or eating out. And the average US pet owner spends more than $2 a day on food, toys, and care for their pet –a family dog or cat in the US consumes more than the world's extremely poor.

But for most of human history, $1.90 was more than the amount that the great majority of people on the planet had to spend. (For most of history we've seen people didn't actually *buy* $1.90 worth of stuff each day, but this was the value of everything they ate or used). Even though they spent about two thirds of what they had on food, it meant most people were hungry a lot of the time. We'll see it meant their houses were awful. They couldn't afford to travel more than a few miles, they couldn't afford light after dark, or books. And they were too poor to be able to have their kids learning in school rather than working in the fields, so childhood ended very young.

That was the life lived by around two thirds of people on the planet when your grandparents were young and about one half when your parents were kids. Today, less than one out of ten people worldwide live on less than $1.90 a day (although the economic slowdown caused by Covid-19 will likely push back progress by four or five years).

Again, most of the nine out of ten people on the planet who live on more than $1.90 a day are still very poor by American standards. But they are at least a bit less poor –and many are a lot less poor– than their parents were.

The last twenty years have seen poorer countries grow richer more rapidly than already rich countries, so that global inequality is falling. But *within* some countries, including the United States, the gap between rich and poor has been growing. Especially the very richest households have seen their incomes skyrocket since your parents were young.

The poorest one fifth of households in the United States have an average income of about $36 per person a day. The richest fifth of households have an income of about $641 per person per a day –eighteen times as much. The poorest households tend to be smaller than the richest, but still, that's a big gap. And the very richest Americans live on tens of thousands of dollars or more a day while there are about 1,265,000 people in America living on less than $4 a day.

Groups that face discrimination in the United States are more likely to be poor. The official US poverty line is set at about $67 a day for a family of four, or $17 for each person. Hispanic Americans see twice the proportion of people living below the official US poverty line than people who describe themselves as white and not Hispanic. African Americans face an even greater chance of living in poverty —one out of every five African American families live below the US official poverty line.

If you were born into a relatively rich family in the United States (and your household is in the top half in America if it makes more than $63,000 a year), you've already won a lottery that will help you the rest of your life. Poorer families in the United States often can't afford to live in the safest neighborhoods or where the best schools are, they often struggle to pay for health care and college. As a result, poorer people in America don't live as long as richer people, they are more likely to be victims of a crime, and their kids don't have the same chance to get to good universities or the best jobs.

America is a country of opportunity, and if you work hard you can achieve a lot —but kids in poorer families must work harder than kids of rich families to achieve the same amount. That's why kids born to wealthy families are far more likely to end up wealthy themselves.

In America, there are a number of government programs with names like the Supplemental Nutritional Assistance Program, or SNAP, that are meant to help the poorest families support their children. There are also programs to pay for housing and health care. Every child can go to school for free and some kids get free meals at school. These programs are one of the things that taxes pay for, and (most) rich people pay more of their income in tax than do poor people. That means the government plays a role in narrowing the gap between poorer and richer people.

But we have seen that gap is still very big. If you think it should be smaller, it would make sense to support more generous programs to help poor people and higher taxes on richer people. You can imagine that idea isn't popular with some rich people.

Looking at global inequality, for all poor countries have been getting richer, there is still a *yawning* gap between the incomes of people in poor and rich countries. Average income per person in the Democratic Republic of the Congo, in central Africa, is $2.30 a day. Compare that to the US poverty line of around $17 a day. And still today we've seen about 700 million people like the Kaburas live in extreme poverty. While that is down from 1,900 million people in 1990, it is still too many.

At the other end of the scale, the world has about 2,000 billionaires. Each one sits on enough money to support someone living on $1.90 a day for nearly 1.5 million years. That's back to the time that our human ancestor homo erectus walked the earth.

And at a planetary level even more than the national level, people are rich or poor because of *where* they are, not *who* they are. Being smart and hardworking helps with financial success but being born to rich parents in America rather than poor parents in places like Burundi helps a lot more. Combined, Jeannine and Arcade Kabura work more than eighty hours a week farming, and on top of that they have to spend fourteen hours a week collecting wood. They aren't lazy, they live in a place where working hard isn't nearly enough to provide for a good quality of life for their children Kathia, Bukur and Butoyi.

Nearer to the US, nearly everyone in Haiti, only about 700 miles from Florida, is poor. Many Haitians must work long hours at backbreaking tasks just to make enough to live. Again, they are poor because of where they are: Haiti just doesn't have many jobs that pay $10 a day, let alone the $7.25 an hour that is the minimum wage in the United States.

That's why most Haitians who live on more than $10 a day don't live in Haiti anymore —they moved. My friends Lant Pritchett and Michael Clemens calculated a few years ago that about 500,000 out of the 600,000 Haitians alive in the world today who live on more than $10 a day live in the United States. That points to one simple thing we can all do to help poor people get richer —let them move to where there are jobs that pay $7.25 an hour.

But we can also help them make more money in their home countries, as well —and make that money go further. Trade helps with both of those things. Trade is just buying and selling stuff across international borders. It means things are made where it is cheap to make them and sold where people want to buy them. People in poor countries can earn more by making stuff to sell in rich countries like the US. They can also buy things from the US that are cheaper to make here than to make there. That way, they have more money to spend to buy things and the things that they buy are cheaper.

Even better, Americans get the same benefits from trade: more money, cheaper things to buy. Trade *really matters* to poor countries, because most of them don't have factories to make cars or trains, medicines, or televisions. They have to buy those products from another country. It also *really matters* to poor people in America, because they spend a lot more of their money on products from other countries than rich people do. Trade helps make both the world and America richer and more equal.

National and global poverty are problems that require governments to fix. If you want to help, you can write to Congressional representatives or the President asking them to provide more assistance to poor families in America and abroad. You can join campaigns calling for better treatment of those who come to America looking for jobs and more opportunities for people in poor countries to buy and sell with the United States on fair terms. United We Dream is one US-based youth-led organization working for immigrant rights and protections which has 400,000 members involved in campaigning and organizing.

But if you want to help more directly, there's a group called Give Directly that does precisely that: it takes your money and gives it straight to some of the poorest families in the world. Those families use it to buy food, medicines, and other necessities. It is an incredibly simple way to reduce poverty. Give Directly understands something very important: the main reason poor people are poor is not a character fault. They are poor because they don't have enough money. And giving people more money helps fix that problem.

People like to argue over whether money makes you happy. Certainly, when you *ask* people if they are happy, lots of people with little money say they are happy, and many rich people say they are miserable. And we will see that the happiness that comes from making another million dollars after you've already got a few million already is pretty small. But when the money we are talking about is money that allows you to buy enough food, to have a safe place to live, to buy the medicines that you need to keep you and your family healthy and not to worry that you won't be able to afford those things tomorrow, then that money really matters – and not having it surely makes for misery. So that less and less of the world faces that kind of poverty is a fantastic thing.

Home

The Kaburas' toilet (Source: Gapminder/Dollar Street)

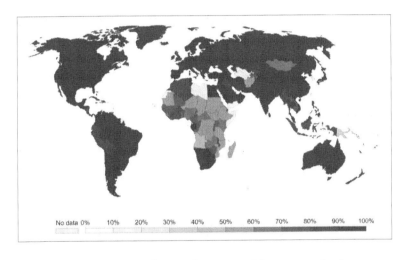

The proportion of people in each country with access to piped or covered well water sources (lighter shades show less coverage) (Source: Our World in Data)

Richard Sclatter was a craftsman in the village of Elmley Castle in England. In 1457, he found himself in trouble with the law and, as part of the court proceedings which followed, a list was made of all his property. Beyond a bit of land and what will probably have been a one-room house with windowless walls made of sticks, mud and manure, all he and his wife had to their names was a table, a chair, a bench, a bed with a sheet, pillows and blanket, a spade, a shovel and a spinning wheel. That, plus some (but not very many) clothes, was typical for the considerable majority of people living in Europe five hundred years ago.

There is a lot in a modern house not on that list: a second chair, more than one bed, any electronics or kitchen appliances. The bathroom was probably a pit or field outside, the sink a stream and the stove and range a wood fire. And unlike Louis XIV of France –but like nearly everyone else– Richard Sclatter certainly wouldn't have been able to afford candles to keep his home lit at night. The sun going down meant darkness.

In my house we've got three toilets, eight faucets on sinks, baths and showers and a whole bunch of different appliances to mix and cook food. We've got computers and tablets, phones and a TV. We've also got about 70 light bulbs that can be turned on with the flick of a switch. If we turned them all on at once it would be the brightness of perhaps 35,000 candles. I'm not sure I would swap my house for Louis XIV's Versailles –let alone for Sclatter's hovel.

Just in the last two generations, the United States has seen a lot of changes in housing and what's in houses. Probably your grandparents had a refrigerator when they were young, but about a fifth of American households did not. Life without a refrigerator involves a lot more shopping for vegetables, milk, and butter as well as a higher tolerance for moldy food. And no frozen pizza, waffles, or ice cream.

About a third of houses didn't have an indoor flush toilet when your grandparents were kids. That means a whole load of people went to the outhouse: a chair with a hole sitting above a pit in the ground with a small wooden shed on top. The 1950s was the decade that the telephone went from being a luxury to something that most people had. Calling 'long distance' –to another state, let alone another country– was still really expensive. Maybe you'd do it for special occasions like a birthday. Most families didn't have a washing machine and that meant hand washing everything –imagine the hours at the sink.

The microwave was an exciting new cooking invention when your parents were young. And only a little more than half of all houses had air conditioning at the time. Doing chores, playing or sleeping in summer all meant sweaty discomfort. Most American households still didn't have a dishwasher.

Planetary progress in housing quality has been even faster –if from a much lower starting point. In 1990, about when your parents were thinking about college, three out of ten households worldwide didn't have electricity. That meant they couldn't watch television, they relied on oil lamps or candles for light, and they certainly couldn't run a refrigerator. Today, that number is closer to one out of ten houses worldwide. When it comes to the kitchen, the share of households that use 'solid fuels' like wood, cow dung, charcoal, or coal for cooking rather than gas or electricity was above six out of ten in 1980, now it is less than four out of ten. We'll see one reason that progress really matters is because of the deadly air pollution produced by fuels like coal, wood, and dung. But it also matters because cooking everything using a fire is time consuming, messy, and takes a lot of effort to collect fuel.

The proportion of the world that has access to clean water –either from a faucet in their house or from a nearby public tap or properly maintained well—has gone up from three quarters in 1990 to nine out of ten in 2015. The proportion of people that have somewhere to go to the toilet where their waste will be safely disposed of –a flush toilet like you have in your house or a well-designed pit latrine– has risen from just above one half in 1990 to above two thirds today.

Back when your parents were young, there were about six telephones for every one hundred people on the planet, and a lot less than that in Africa and Asia. Telephones were a luxury for city dwellers and most people will never have used one. There are now more mobile phone numbers in use worldwide than there are people. That doesn't mean everyone has access to a mobile phone, but most people do. And about eight out of ten households have a television. More than half of the world now uses the Internet –up from pretty much nobody when your parents were college-aged.

We talked in the last chapter about the fact that how much money people have has increased over time, but both advances in health and comforts at home demonstrate that people's choice of what to buy with that money has also gone up a lot: they can buy mobile phones and TVs and microwave cookers and drugs for high blood pressure that even the richest people couldn't afford when your grandparents were born –because those things hadn't been invented yet.

And technology advance means some things – lighting, televisions, and mobile phones in particular—have got a LOT cheaper. To earn enough to buy a candle that could provide an hour's light would take six hours of work in England in 1800. In 1950 it took eight seconds of work to buy an hour's light from an incandescent light bulb (which works by running electricity through a wire to get it hot enough to glow). For a modern bulb today, it takes a tiny fraction of a second.

Again, governments have got better at providing basic services like electricity connections and piped sewage systems to everyone –rich and poor. Still, there is a long way to go before everyone in America –let alone the world- lives in a decent house.

In the United States, many people live in homes with more people than rooms –about 2,564,000 households. According to the US Census Bureau, more than fifteen million houses were home to cockroaches in 2017 while more than two million homes had been without a working flush toilet at some point in the last three months. Nearly four million houses had mold. And a lot of people in America –about half a million on the average night in 2018– don't have a house at all. They are homeless. About seven in ten of those people find a space in a shelter. Many of the rest are living on the streets.

Worldwide, still more than 700 million people lack access to clean water and more than a third of the world still lacks a decent place to go to the toilet, with many simply using the nearest field. Even more are still using dirty fuels like wood and dung to cook, endangering their health with the smoke and soot. Especially amongst the world's poorest people, very few own a television or a bicycle (let alone a car or a computer). Their houses often have only one room. That pretty much describes the living conditions of the Kabura family from Burundi: a one room hut with a leaking roof and a dirt floor; heat, light and cooking all from a wood fire in the middle of the hut; no table or chairs; and a covered pit outside as a toilet (pictured at the start of the chapter).

What's the answer to those problems? The shortest one is 'money.' It costs money to build a house, it costs money to furnish it, and companies or governments need money to dig holes, lay pipes and provide water, sewage, and electricity services. Once again, a big thing you can do to help is ask your government –your state representatives and senators, your federal representatives—to provide more money so that more people who don't have decent housing or decent electricity and water can get it here in the US and worldwide.

But if you want to get more directly involved, Habitat for Humanity is an organization that helps families build and improve homes here in the US and in other countries. And homeless shelters in your community need support: your time to help prepare and serve meals, and your money to buy that food.

Still, a growing number of people worldwide have somewhere to call home that is more than simply a small and inadequate shelter against the weather. Home has become considerably safer thanks to electricity and sewage systems. It has become more comfortable thanks to better building materials, more furniture, and more space. And home has become more entertaining thanks to more toys, books, games, and electronics. Most of us have no excuse to be bored any more. And that is another way the world has gotten better.

School

Jan Steen's "A School for Boys and Girls" (1670). Still better than Zoom classes? (Source: Wikimedia)

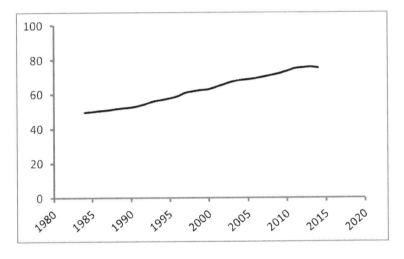

The percentage of children worldwide who complete lower secondary education —middle school or junior high.

In 1670, the Dutch artist Jan Steen painted a picture of "A School for Boys and Girls". The school is one big room, and there are what looks like 26 kids from pre-K to pre-teens in it, along with two teachers. It doesn't look like much learning is going on. One of the teachers is helping a boy with reading, and perhaps four more kids are paying attention to that. A couple more may be studying by themselves. As to the other nineteen: two kids appear to be trying to persuade the class owl to try on a pair of glasses; one child is asleep on the floor; one is dancing on a table; two more are fighting; and a bunch of kids are watching the mayhem and laughing. The room is a mess —a tobacco pipe is smoldering on the flagstones along with a bunch of vegetables, pictures, cups, leaves, bags, books and a bucket. One of the tables is tipped over. And the second teacher is sat back in his chair, carving a pen nib and seemingly oblivious to it all.

Steen was a painter with a sense of humor, so it isn't fair to suggest his picture represents the average school in Seventeenth Century Holland. But it is probably safe to say the quality of education was lower than we expect nowadays.

Despite that, the Netherlands was a leader in schooling at the time. Perhaps four out of five young men could read, although the rate amongst young women was lower. Connecticut and the Massachusetts Bay Colony were also ahead on education: they mandated universal elementary schooling in the 1640s and 50s. But nearly everywhere else on the planet, education was optional and limited to those very few who could afford it. The vast majority of people through the vast majority of history have been unable to read and write.

Education may be one of the things in America that looks like it has changed least in the last 60 years since your parents and grandparents were young. I go into my kids' schools and even some of the smells remind me of time I spent in a middle school in Minnesota around 1980 (not always in a good way). The corridors and lockers look the same, and the classrooms are set up the same way. Still, there are more chrome books and electronics around along with fewer blackboards –and if you ask your teachers, they will tell you everything really isn't the same: the way they teach has changed a lot.

That is why when children ask their parents to help with their homework the constant reply is: "they didn't teach it like that when I was a kid." (Of course, there is a *chance* they have simply forgotten, but they would argue it is small).

And more people spend more time in school than a half-century ago. If you look at what American 18- and 19-year-olds were doing in 1970, about one in six had left high school before getting their diploma. A bit more than a third were in college. Today, only about one out of every fourteen have left school before getting their high school diploma while about half are already in college. And if you look at total college enrollment, about a quarter of people aged between 18 and 24 were in college in 1980, compared to about two fifths today. Women were about a third of the people going to college in America in 1950, half by 1979, and by 2019 there were more women than men in college in the United States.

Worldwide, the change has been dramatic over the past few decades as poor countries have hugely expanded school enrollment. You may know the story of Malala Yousafzai. At the age of twelve, she began campaigning for the right of girls to go to school –something she had been denied when extremists in her district of Pakistan had banned girls' education and destroyed a bunch of girls' schools. Three years later, when she was riding a bus near her home, she was shot in the head by one of the extremists. She survived and has gone on to lead a global campaign for the right to education. It was a horrible attack, but that it shocked the world is in some ways a sign of how much global attitudes to education —and, in particular, girls' education– have changed.

And as amazing as was Malala's bravery before and after the attack, so was the bravery and commitment shown by children (and their parents) who followed her lead. Although still today fewer girls are in school in Malala's home district than boys, the gap is shrinking –and more children boys and girls alike are attending school. In your grandparents' time, across much of the world, most kids didn't go to school —and most of those few who did were boys. Today things look very different.

The decade your grandparents were born was about the time that we went from a minority to a majority of the world being able to read an easy sentence. By the time your parents were born it was closer to two thirds of the world. Now, it is about nine out of ten. In 1970, a little before your parents were born, 960 million people older than the age of fifteen had completed elementary school worldwide —less than half of the total adult population. 101 million, or about one in every twenty, had gone to college. By 2020, about 3,251 million people fifteen years old or older worldwide completed elementary school —about three quarters of them. 842 million, or about one in five, had gone to college. The world has eight times more college graduates than it did when your parents were young and three times more people who have finished elementary school.

That's a lot more people who have the basic skills to become the next Maya Angelou, Bill Gates, Marie Curie or Albert Einstein. In Burundi, where the Kabura family live, only about a quarter of kids who should have been in elementary school were in school in the 1970s, more than nine out of ten are today.

There is still a long way to go. A little less than 300,000 American kids each year drop out before they finish high school. Over time it has become harder and harder for people without a high school diploma to get a decent job, so those kids are going to have a hard time as adults. And a lot of those who start college don't finish –it is harder to get a good job for those people, too. Again, while women have more than closed the education gap with men, minority groups and poorer families still see lower rates of college completion. Compared to about a third of the total population that has a bachelor's degree, the proportion is closer to a fifth for African Americans and less than a sixth for Hispanic Americans.

Worldwide, in the year 2014, about 61 million kids who should have been in elementary school weren't in school. That's 39 million less than in 2000, and the gap between girls and boys had dropped by two thirds, to 3 million children. But it is still a lot of people. And more school-age children worldwide aren't in middle school or high school: about 201 million. Chances are pretty slim that the Kabura kids (Kathia, Bukur and Butoyi) will complete high school. Many of those out of school are working in fields or trying to sell things on the side of the highway. Others are raising sisters, brothers, or their own kids. Few are on the path towards a high standard of living.

Almost as bad as not being in school, there are millions of students sitting in school learning nothing year after year. In many places in the world, if you fall behind your classmates and can't keep up with the lessons, they don't give you extra help or maybe suggest you repeat a grade, they just stick you in the next grade regardless, and you fall ever further behind. That means many children leave fifth grade knowing little more than they did in first or second.

Sometimes the quality of the education children are receiving doesn't look that different from what you can see in Jan Steen's painting. A survey of schools and classrooms in Nigeria found that one fifth of classes had no teacher there at all, the average teacher only got about a fifth of questions right on a test of dividing two fractions, and there were more than three students for every textbook.

Beyond staying in school, working hard and being grateful towards your teachers, what can you do to make things better? Mentoring programs can really help younger kids who are falling behind –if you can help now or in a few years, that is a fantastic thing to do.

You could help support a school in a developing country and learn about life there through twinning programs where you have hangouts and email with kids from that school. You could support the work of the Malala Fund, which works to ensure all girls are in school. And you can tell your Senators and Representatives that you want everyone to be able to go to school worldwide, and that the government should support that by providing more support for quality education from pre-K through college in the US, more support for people from other countries to come to American colleges, and assistance to education systems in the developing world.

Some of what you learn in school, you may never use again. I learned a LOT about the British canal system of the 1850s and it hasn't often come in handy in my job or at home. That said, I learned how to learn, and learned lots of things that I *have* used after leaving school: from how to read a graph to how to spot a weak argument.

Education is the only thing that stops humans starting again, every generation, from what we knew when we were newly evolved from apes in the jungle, with nothing but instinct to guide us. The reason humanity keeps on progressing is that we both discover new things and pass that knowledge on to the next generation: how to build a generator or an engine, how to manufacture a lightbulb or design a tax system, how to paint using perspective and how to run a fair trial. That more and more people can learn more and more stuff is essential to the world getting better.

Work and Leisure

Women harvest a potato crop by hand, Kansas, 1941. Imagine doing this all day. And then doing it again tomorrow. (Source: Wikimedia)

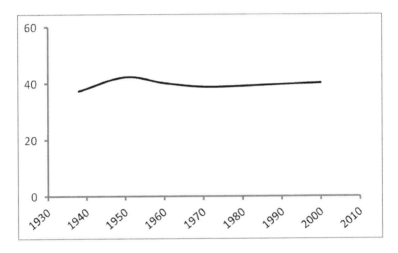

Weekly working hours for the full-time employed in the US.
Spot the trend?

As Covid-19 spread around the world in 2020, a lot of places closed their borders to travelers. That was a real problem for farmers in many richer countries, who rely on visiting workers from poorer countries to provide the help they need to tend and harvest crops. The call went up for local people who had lost jobs working in restaurants or offices to fill in and save the crops. In the UK, 50,000 people initially applied for jobs as fruit pickers. But then they discovered more about the work: out in all weather for eight hours a day doing backbreaking labor. Only about 100 of the applicants actually ended up helping on farms. There were similar stories across Europe and the United States: people used to serving coffees or punching keys were utterly unprepared and unwilling to do farm work.

That suggests they were incredibly lucky to be living in a rich country in the Twenty First Century rather than any other place or time, because for most of history, nearly everyone had no choice but to take the same job: farming. Their labor was dedicated to producing enough to feed themselves and their family and a little on top paid as tithes, tribute, or tax –or simply taken from them if they were slaves.

Some people spent most of their time tending animals, most people spent most of their time growing plants. Crops varied around the world, and tools too. Some farmers used oxen, cattle or horses to plough fields, in other places or other times pretty much all of the labor was done by hand. But nearly everywhere, the work would begin soon after dawn and finish around dusk. It would start for children as soon as they were capable and end only with death or disability. Sometimes, the monotony would be broken by a day off –in some parts of the world, Sundays were for prayer, feast days for small celebration. Song and dance, storytelling and sports have always been around. But days were long, nights were dark, work was hard and vacations a luxury for a tiny elite.

By the time your grandparents were born, the United States had already gone through a massive shift in what people did for a living. In the early 1960s, only about two or three out of every 100 Americans worked on a farm. Since then, it has fallen further –from four million to two million people, or a little more than one percent of the working population. Around when your grandparents were born, about one third of people worked in manufacturing, mostly in factories, making stuff. By the time your parents were born that was down to about a quarter and today it is one in ten.

That means the great majority of people working in the US today don't earn a living by making or growing physical stuff. Instead, their jobs involve helping other people: educating, informing, entertaining, and healing them, keeping them safe or moving them around, selling them things that others have made or dealing with their money. This kind of work is grouped under the label 'services' by economists and it covers jobs from pharmacist and lawyer through teacher and comedian to sanitation worker and soldier.

In the US, ever fewer people are working as replacements for something that could be done by a dumb machine, because dumb machines are doing that work instead. People don't dig and turn the soil to plant new crops except as part of a hobby, tractors pulling ploughs do that. People don't pound wet clothes against a rock to get them clean, they stick them in the washing machine. People don't fill a box with 60 cookies on an assembly line, three boxes a minute for eight hours a day, a robot does that. That change is a huge factor behind growing prosperity, but also towards a more interesting life at work. Digging up a field of potatoes isn't only back breaking, it is mind-numbing.

Instead of working in the fields or on assembly lines in factories, people are doing a bunch of jobs that simply didn't exist when your grandparents were young (software engineer, for example). And as well as there being more different and more interesting types of jobs, work is getting safer.

People working on farms, in mines and in factories often work with dangerous equipment: threshers, drills, stamping machines. In contrast, it is *really hard* to get seriously physically hurt when typing on a keyboard. And while restaurant kitchens can be dangerous places, they aren't nearly as bad as a mine shaft. That will be one reason why people don't die on the job as much as they used to. In the 1940s, about thirty people died at work for every 100,000 people working in the United States. That's now down to an average of about four deaths each year for each 100,000 people working.

People spend less of their life at work, too. At the younger end, they enter the workforce later because they're spending more time at school and college. They spend more time in retirement because they are living longer. Perhaps as importantly, the *quality* of time away from work has improved.

That's most obvious with home entertainment. Cable TV got more popular as your parents grew up, but for most families who didn't have it at the start of the 1980s, there were just three network TV channels. There were only three shows you could watch at any one time on those channels. And you had to watch them when they were on –late home from school? Too bad, you missed it.

Although, to be honest, you weren't missing much. Family shows included *CHiPs*, *Happy Days*, and *The Waltons*. It might be worth viewing some clips on YouTube to see what you think of their quality. Meanwhile, almost nobody had a computer at home and absolutely no-one had an i-Pad or a Kindle, or a mobile phone that could do anything but make a voice call. The Internet hadn't been invented. Pretty much the only video game was called Pong –again, you can play a version online. It involves bouncing a white glowing electronic square 'ball' back and forth between two 'paddles' that could only move up and down in a line. That's it: two-dimensional ping-pong with one-dimensional paddle control.

But it isn't just video games and TV shows: anyone with access to the Internet can download almost any book they want from a local library or online collection; or look at millions of quality images of the greatest works of art; or find out about almost anything from Wikipedia; or video chat with friends the world over, all for free.

A lot more people are leaving home on holidays to experience new places and meet new people in real life, as well (the Covid-19 restrictions marking a sad but temporary reversal). In the 1960s, fewer than one in five Americans had ever set foot on a plane, for example. Today that's closer to nine out of ten.

The trend towards better work and more leisure is global. Worldwide, the proportion of all employed people who work on farms has fallen from more than two fifths to about a quarter just since 1991, around when your parents started working. About another quarter work in industry –factories and mines, for example. More than half the world works in services. Automation is spreading everywhere.

And the average age at which people start working is rising. About one quarter of the world's children aged 10 to 14 years old were working in the 1950s, when your grandparents were young. By 1980s, when your parents were kids, that was down to a fifth. Now it is below a tenth. The worldwide workweek has also converged to forty hours–nine to five.

Both cable TV and the Internet have spread very rapidly: about half the people in the world have used the Internet in the past three months. And global tourism is on the rise: there were about 500 million international tourist trips taken in 1995, that's up to over a billion and a quarter recently (again, with 2020 being a sad exception).

The quality of work and the quality of leisure are both closely related to the strength of a country's economy. The most reliable way to predict how many people will be in reasonably well-paying jobs with good conditions is to look at a country's wealth: rich countries usually have better jobs.

That said, in the United States and worldwide a lot of people remain in jobs that are miserable: suffering bad working conditions, little or no time off, toiling for low pay, constantly worried they might be fired. Many others can't find a job at all. During good times for the economy, one in twenty people in the US who want to work can't find employment. In bad times, that climbs above one in ten. (In the midst of the Covid-19 pandemic in 2020 it reached near one in seven).

Worldwide, most of those working in agriculture are still there by lack of option more than by choice, often farming without the help of a single engine to run a tractor or pump. And most people across the planet working in industry and services are in the 'informal economy' —laws on working conditions and hours don't cover them, and they aren't guaranteed a living wage.

In a few of the world's poorest countries, still more than half of all children aged between seven and fourteen are working, most of them on farms –like the Kaburas of Burundi. In Bangladesh, a few years ago, six out of ten children were working, each for an average of 32 hours a week. Many of their parents face the choice between putting the children to work or having them suffer (worse) poverty and malnourishment.

And, worldwide, there is still a lot of discrimination in who gets the best jobs –or who gets paid to work at all. For every four men in paid work in the United States there are only three women. Across the planet, the proportion is about two women to every three men. The women who aren't being paid aren't sitting back and toggling buttons on their gaming consoles, the vast majority are doing unpaid work. In particular, and on average, women with young families still spend a lot more time caring for their children than men do. For all it may be labor of love, it is still labor. It may be hard to believe, but kids can be immensely frustrating to deal with, sometimes.

Once the children are old enough to look after themselves, women tend to go back to less well-paid jobs than their partners who haven't taken time away from their careers, which means the 'child penalty' of pay and job status sticks for life. Again, blacks and Latinos with the same qualifications as white job applicants are hired less often in the US, mirroring worldwide discrimination against minority groups.

The picture is far from perfect when it comes to time away from work, as well. For all the growth in leisure time, *you* may not see much of it for another fifty or sixty years. In the US, average working hours for a full-time employee fell from about 60 hours 100 years ago closer to 40 hours by 1960, but there they stuck. And the amount of time people spend in leisure −not at work or school, not doing housework or commuting or taking a shower or bath—was 42 hours in 1940, 42 hours in 1970 and around 41 hours when you were born. Leisure has actually declined for teenagers over that time:

your grandparents had it easier as kids at least in that sense.

And the US still doesn't mandate that employers give people *any* paid vacation days and holidays. That makes America different from almost every other country in the world. By law, people in Germany get a minimum of 33 days off a year, for example. In fact, despite the lack of legal requirements, the average American worker gets about ten vacation days and six holidays (set days off like Memorial Day and Labor Day). But that's still less than half the legal minimum in Germany. And for the lowest-paid workers, the average is just eight days of vacation and holiday combined. Of course, for the great majority of people in the developing world, there is simply no such thing as 'paid time off.'

When it comes to spending that leisure time, older people also worry about how younger people —and especially their own kids—use it. 'Too much screen time' is probably the most common parental concern of this century in rich countries. I worry about it, too, but it is worth noting that your grandparents' generation complained endlessly about the time your parents wasted watching television. Similar angst surrounded the radio earlier in the Twentieth Century and the evils of reading novels in the Nineteenth Century. If the past is a guide, those of you who become parents will end up admonishing your own children about the hours they are spending in virtual reality, distracting them from finishing an important school assignment studying Tik-Toks.

Fixing the world of work is a complex challenge for kids at school. But one way to help in the longer term is to learn a lot in school and then become a generous and understanding manager or owner. And don't waste your leisure time sitting around complaining that you are bored. Meanwhile, there are groups that work to help ensure the things that you buy aren't made by people working in terrible conditions abroad, and you can follow their advice on where to shop —the Clean Clothes Campaign and the Fairtrade movement are both examples.

Or you could support youth-led movements in countries where child labor is still common. The African Movement of Working Children and Youth operates in 27 countries with about 270,955 active members, most under the age of 18. They meet in local groups that provide support to members in times of need and work together to further twelve child rights: to read and write; to express yourself; to be taught a trade; to play and have leisure; to have health care; to be listened to; to rest when sick; to work in safety; to be respected and have dignity; to stay in the village; to do light and limited work; and to have access to equitable justice.

You will spend a huge chunk of your life at work. It is great that the choice of work you do, and the likelihood you well be safe and well paid doing it, has never been higher. The US has a long way to go to ensure everyone who wants one has a good job, though –and the world as a whole, much further still.

War and Violence

The Battle of Crecy: Part of the Hundred Year's War during which two million people died in fighting over which set of nobles got to assault and exploit French peasants (Source: Wikimedia)

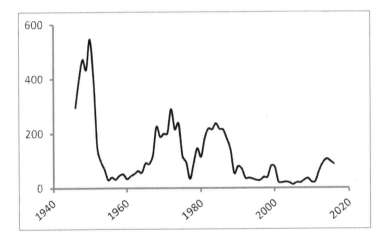

Yearly deaths in battle worldwide since 1946, in thousands

The Hundred Years' War was a conflict between England and France that actually lasted 116 years. To be fair, they took breaks. The years 1360 to 1369, for example, were reasonably peaceful –in part because the French king spent a lot of that time as a hostage in England. But, pretty much, 1337 to 1453 was over a century of bloody conflict over French lands and who should rule them that killed 2 million people or more.

For the average English or French subject, the war was an utter waste of lives, time and money. And that was hardly the exception: the great majority of wars in history may have led to the glory of a victorious royal and some barons and lords, perhaps the exchange of land and the people who live on it, but it has involved little but suffering and death for those people themselves.

And many conflicts were far more deadly than the Hundred Years War: nineteen hundred years ago, China's War of the Three Kingdoms killed more than 30 million people, for example. So, it is a wonderful thing that not only war, but violence in general, has been declining recently. In fact, over the very long term, violence has gone from a major cause of death to a comparatively rare and tragic event across most of the world.

About the time your grandparents were thinking about having kids, the US introduced a lottery to help decide which Americans would have to fight in the Vietnam War –a conflict that pitted the communist North of the country against a government supported by the US in the South. There were not enough volunteers in the United States to join the army, so a system was set up to compel people into uniform. In 1971, the 365 days of the year were written down on pieces of paper and stuck in a barrel, which was spun around for an hour. A second drum had papers with numbers from 1 to 365 written on them. That barrel was spun around, too. At the end of the hour, the pieces of paper from both barrels were pulled out one after the other. The dates from one barrel were matched to a number from the other. July 9th got number one. That meant any man born on July 9th, 1951, was first in line to be drafted –made to join the army if he wanted to or not.

More than 2 million American men were drafted to fight the Vietnam War –a conflict that killed 57,000 American troops and more than one million Vietnamese soldiers and civilians. The communists ended up winning, which likely would have been the result had the Americans stayed at home. But a lot fewer people would have died in the meantime.

There was a lot of violence back home in America as well around the time when your parents were born. During the 1970s, groups including Symbionese Liberation Army kidnapped people for ransom, and 112 US planes were hijacked. The Civil Rights leader Martin Luther King and Robert Kennedy, a Democratic candidate for the presidency, were both shot and killed in 1968. King's assassination led to massive riots in cities including Washington DC, Chicago, and Baltimore. And the overall murder rate peaked at about one killed for each 10,000 Americans each year in the 1970s.

Of course, the United States is still fighting wars —most recently in countries including Afghanistan and Iraq. More than 14,000 US soldiers and contract fighters have died in those two conflicts since they began, along with around

100,000 Iraqi and Afghan troops, about the same number of opposition fighters, and 250,000 Afghan and Iraqi civilians. But it is still safer to be a US soldier today than it was in the 1990s –let alone the 1970s: the risk of dying from enemy action or accidents is less than it has ever been.

And for those of us not in the military, life is even safer still. The murder rate in the United States is now about half of the level it was in the 1970s, 80s and 90s. Your risk of dying in a terror attack in the US is a lot less than your risk of dying from a bee sting or drowning in the bath (both of which are *extremely* unlikely). Again, hate crimes against minorities and violence against women have both been declining in the US over the past thirty years.

The chance that a person is murdered in the United States today is less than the chance of flipping a coin and getting heads, doing it again, and again, and again, and again, and again, and again, and again, and again, and again, and again, and again, and again, and again —that's heads 14 times in a row. And the chance is less than that for kids under the age of 14 –add two more coin flips, for a total of 16 heads in a row. Violence in this country is far too high, and we should make it much rarer. But it is still already rare. In terms of risk, most people should be more worried about things like not texting while they are crossing the street so that they don't get run over.

Again, most children practice lockdowns at school because sometimes, rarely, people try to hurt kids there. But school is still one of the safest places to be in –with teachers, police and parents working to make sure students are protected. And criminally violent acts in US schools like assault have gotten rarer just in the past twenty years –from about one case for every 100 students over the age of twelve in 1993 to about one for every 500 students in 2015.

Looking worldwide, at around the time your grandparents were born, the Korean War was being fought. That was a major reason why more than 546,000 people died in battle planet-wide in 1950. As we have seen, around when your parents were born, the Vietnam War was raging and about 290,000 died in battle in 1972. The tragic conflict in Syria over the last few years has been responsible for hundreds of thousands of deaths, and 105,000 people died on the battlefield worldwide in 2014 –

the worst recent year of violence. But as these numbers make clear, the trend has been towards a lower number of deaths. An average person's annual risk of dying in battle worldwide has fallen from one chance in 5,000 in 1950 to one chance in 85,000 in 2016.

The amount we spend on war is also going down. At the start of the decade in which your parents were born, one out of every $20 of the world's income was used to fund armies, navies and air forces. Today that is closer to one out of every $46. The United States spent about one out of every $13 of its income on the military in 1970 compared to one out of every $32 today. That means it is spending more than the average country, but still less than a few decades ago.

Through history —and today— far more people worldwide have died violent deaths off the battlefield than on it. Governments themselves have been a major cause. Genocides —mass murder of people based on their skin color, culture, or religion- have killed many millions in the last century. Thankfully, genocides have become less common in the last few decades. The risk of murder has also dropped dramatically over history. Typical murder rates in Europe in medieval times were more than twenty times their level today. More recently, the murder rate has been falling around the world, at least since the 1990s. In India, the risk of being murdered fell from one chance in 22,000 in 1991 to one chance in 35,000 in 2010.

There is an argument over what accounts for the decline of war and murder worldwide, and if it will continue. But people are turning against the idea of all sorts of physical violence. We used to torture animals for fun in circuses and bull fights, now that is dying out. Hunting as a sport is becoming less popular. The proportion of parents in the US who disagree with the idea of spanking children as a punishment increased from one out of six in 1986 to one out of three in 2016.

Worldwide, the number of countries that use the death penalty for any crime has dramatically fallen. In the mid-1970s, about 20 countries had banned the death penalty. By the mid-1990s, that had climbed to around 60 and by 2010 to over 100. The number of people worldwide who say they wouldn't fight for their country is growing. No-one thinks countries should fight a war for glory or slaves anymore, and ever fewer people think it is right to fight a war for resources or land.

One factor behind all these changed attitudes may be the other, better, ways to riches and glory. In the past, taking someone else's land or their gold was a great way to wealth —but you might have to kill them to take it. Nowadays, the more reliable way for people and countries to get rich is to make and sell new stuff rather than taking old stuff. And people and countries who rely on selling things do better when the world is peaceful than when it is at war. Meanwhile, for the rest of us, the risk of getting into a fight and getting killed didn't look as bad if we might have died of smallpox the next day anyway. But now a peaceful life can last for 80 years or more, getting into a fight looks ever more stupid and risky.

Beyond changing attitudes, good policing in countries and cooperation between them has also played a big role in reducing global violence. Within countries, people are less likely to get away with murder than they used to be. And internationally, the United Nations can cut countries off from trade or put together alliances to respond if one country attacks another. Peacekeepers —soldiers lent to the United Nations so that it can end wars and maintain stability—have played a big part in controlling conflict in countries in Europe, Asia, the Middle East and Africa.

The world is still far from utterly peaceful. One third of children aged 13 to 15 in the United States report they were in a physical fight last year at school. Again, America remains a lot more violent than most rich countries. The chance of being murdered in the US is ten times the risk in the Germany. A big part of the difference is due to easy access to guns in America. American households own more guns than there are people in the country. That compares to about one gun for every five people in Germany.

And in some countries, a lot of children report being physically punished by teachers —more than three quarters of all children aged eight in India, for example. Often, the teachers aren't breaking the law: sixty-nine countries allow school staff to use physical violence to discipline children. Reports of fighting and bullying are even more frequent than in the US. Again, in India, about one quarter of women between the ages of 15 and 49 report their partner —usually a boyfriend or husband—has physically attacked them in the past year, part of a worldwide epidemic of household violence.

More seriously still, the risk of being murdered in countries including India, Italy and the United States is still only about the same as when your grandparents were born —the 1950s were also a low-point in homicide rates. In some countries in Central America in particular, a growing number of people are victims of violence, much of it related to the illegal drug trade.

Looking at weapons of war, although about one sixth the number in the 1980s, the world still contains more than 10,000 nuclear weapons —still quite enough to end human civilization.

And ongoing conflict in Afghanistan, Yemen, South Sudan, and Syria is creating widespread misery alongside deaths. It has also created a wave of refugees escaping the violence —part of a total 25,900,000 people worldwide who have fled their home countries.

What can you do to help reduce violence and help those suffering the consequences? At school, you should report any violence you see. You can support campaigns to reduce the number of the deadliest guns on America's streets through groups like Students Demand Action for Gun Sense. You can work with organizations pushing for international agreements to reduce the number of weapons countries sell to each other, like the International Campaign to Ban Landmines. You can write to your Congressional representatives arguing for more support to United Nations peacekeeping missions.

For the people who are forced to leave their own countries because of war or violence, you can help them by welcoming them into your communities. Older refugees need somewhere safe to live and work. Younger refugees need to go to school, and they need friends. There are many local groups that help refugees settle into new homes – think about volunteering with one of them.

People wounding and killing other people has been a tragic constant of human history. But it is happening less than it used to. Violence to gain advantage or win a dispute is going out of fashion, and the world is a more friendly place as a result.

Freedom from Discrimination

Sir Hugh Le Despencer has his stomach slit open for the crimes of treason, heresy and being gay: fourteenth century official punishment and spectator sport. (Source: Wikimedia)

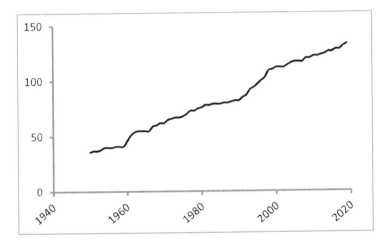

The number of countries worldwide where being gay or lesbian isn't considered a crime.

Sir Hugh Le Despencer was a Royal Chamberlain to Edward II, king of England. When Edward was deposed by his wife Queen Isabella, Spencer was brought to trial. Doubtless guilty of real crimes, he was actually convicted of treason, heresy (believing things not accepted by the church) and having sex with men. He was dragged through the streets, hung by the neck until nearly dead, then his stomach was split open and his intestines pulled out. Subsequently, he was beheaded and finally his body cut into four pieces.

Beyond an example of how much governments used to carry out acts of obscene punishment, Spencer's 'crimes' included at least two behaviors that are no longer considered criminal at all in England: being gay and not being a 'proper' Christian. That helps illustrate that the freedom of choice that most people enjoy today –in what to believe, and what to do—is hugely more than the freedom enjoyed by most people through history. It is also a sign that discrimination on the grounds of features of birth –gender, skin color, sexual orientation—has declined.

When your grandparents were young, 'Jim Crow' laws in America's South kept African Americans at the back of the bus and in worse schools, and limited their rights to vote. It was only in 1964 that the Civil Rights Act banned discrimination in restaurants, hotels, stores and workplaces, which meant that African Americans wouldn't be served or couldn't work in the same places under the same rules as white people. And it was only in 1967, a little before your parents were born, that the US Supreme Court said that states could not ban marriages between white and black people.

In 1970, a quarter of white adult Americans still said that black and white kids should go to separate schools. More than that said they would move to a new house if a black family moved in next door. Now, hardly anyone is willing to say such things to pollsters. In 1970, more than half of Americans were still in favor of laws banning marriage between whites and blacks. In 1995, when your parents were probably already adults, still less than half of white Americans said they were in favor of white people and black people marrying. But by 2013, that had reached more than four out of five. And the proportion of marriages that are between people who identify themselves as from different races or ethnicities climbed from one in fifteen to one in seven between 1980 and 2010.

Same sex marriage was still illegal in most of the country when you were born: the US Supreme Court only said that it was a right of all Americans in 2015. In 1996, when your parents were already adults, only a quarter of all Americans thought that gays and lesbians should have the right to marry. Today the proportion is about two thirds. In 1987, more than half of all Americans thought schools should have the right to fire gay or lesbian teachers. By 2012, that had dropped to one out of five. In 1977, only one in seven people thought gays and lesbians should be able to adopt children, now three quarters believe they should.

Again, when US adults were surveyed in 1945 and asked, "do you approve of a married woman working if her husband can support her?" less than one in five Americans said that they approved. By 1985 that had reached above four fifths. The proportion of women working increased from less than a third to over one half in that time and is now around six out of every ten women (although we have seen that is still lower than for men, where about seven out of ten are working). In 1975, 62 percent of Americans said they would prefer a man as a boss compared to 7 percent who would prefer a woman (31 percent suggested no preference). By 2017, that had changed to 23 percent saying they would rather have a man as a boss to 21 percent saying they would rather have a woman and 56 percent suggesting no preference. The United States is —all too slowly—becoming less racist and sexist, and less discriminatory against lesbians, gays, and transgender people.

The trends in the United States are reflected in global progress towards greater freedom and less discrimination. Slavery was legal pretty much everywhere a few hundred years ago and only ended in 1980, in your parents' lifetime, when Mauritania became the last country in the world to ban it. For much of history, even people who weren't slaves lacked basic rights —to leave where they lived without permission of their lord, to worship a different god, to say what they thought about politics, to do the job they wanted to do or even to wear the clothes they wanted to wear. Nearly all the world's countries now say people should have these rights, even if in reality many people still face discrimination and persecution.

In 1950, more than four out of five countries had laws that discriminated against ethnic minorities, like America's Jim Crow legislation. By 1980 that was still above one third, but it had dropped below one fifth by 2000. Three quarters of all countries had discriminatory legal constraints against women in 1960 –banning them from driving trains or opening bank accounts without a male guardian's permission for example. Today more than one half of countries have removed all of those barriers.

In the 1960s, homosexuality (being gay or lesbian) was branded as illegal in about three quarters of the world's countries. By 1990 that had dropped to about three out of five. Today it is closer to one third of countries. Attitudes have changed, too. In the last 30 years the proportion of the world that says they do not want to live next to a gay or lesbian person has dropped from three out of five to around one half –700 million fewer people worldwide hold this discriminatory attitude than would be expected given attitudes thirty years ago.

Kids have also gained freedoms –not least, to have a childhood. We've seen child labor is slowly dying out, and fewer children are being married off by their parents before they reach adulthood (the proportion dropped from a quarter to a fifth of all children over the past ten years). Perhaps this helps put homework, screen time limits and bedtimes in perspective.

Millions of acts of bravery help to account for these global changes. For example, in 2011, Manal al-Sharif drove her car from a café to a grocery store, where she picked up some treats for her son before driving back to the café. Her friend Wajeha was in the passenger seat and made a video of the drive on her i-Phone. This utterly unremarkable activity was an act of defiance because Manal al-Sharif's drive took place in Saudi Arabia, where it was against the law for women to drive in 2011. She was arrested two days later and spent ten days in jail. Another woman who protested by driving on the same day was sentenced to be whipped. Others were only released when their husbands or fathers signed a pledge that they would never allow the same thing to happen again. But more and more women went for a drive in Saudi Arabia, and uploaded videos of themselves doing it. By 2017, the government had relented: it became legal for a woman to drive a car. This kind of nonviolent protest is a huge part of the reason that the world is becoming freer: people risking punishment by refusing to be un-free.

In the US, it was an act of immense bravery when six-year-old Ruby Bridges walked quietly toward William Frantz Elementary in Louisiana as the first black child to go to the previously all-white school in November 1960. She was surrounded by federal marshals to protect her from a mob of protesters. Once she got inside, all but one of the teachers refused to teach her, and she spent the whole year in a class of one, most days facing threats and jeers as she walked to school. But she stayed, graduated, and went on to have two schools named after her.

More broadly, economic and social change helps: richer more peaceful countries where people have spent longer in school usually protect rights better than poorer countries where fewer people have gone to high school or college. And the United Nations plays a role: the Universal Declaration of Human Rights bans slavery and torture, and demands equal treatment by the law, the right to a trial if accused of breaking the law, the freedom of movement within countries and the right to leave, freedom of belief and opinion, the right to equal pay for equal work, and the right to education. The United Nations has helped create an expectation that these rights will be honored and (usually) calls out countries that abuse them. Worldwide communication is another factor. For example, in 2020, the Black Lives Matter protests went global, with 4,079 different cities and towns across every continent from Tromso in Northern Norway to Fiji in the South Pacific.

Even though human rights are proclaimed more than ever, they are still abused everywhere. The last few years have demonstrated how far America has to go, and why the Black Lives Matter protests were so important: in 2017, blacks represented 12% of the U.S. adult population but 33% of the sentenced prison population, reflecting a whole range of different elements of discrimination from jobs, housing and schooling through policing and sentencing.

There are still Americans who see African Americans and Hispanics as second-class citizens, who don't think women should have the same opportunities as men —or at least don't act that way (a big reason why only about one in ten of the world's billionaires are women). There are Americans who would deny freedoms to gays and lesbians that are granted to heterosexual people, who don't want to work with people in wheelchairs, or socialize with people who have different religious beliefs —the list goes on. That discrimination means (at the least) women and minorities must work harder than white cisgender non-disabled men to do well in life. All too often, it means they remain subject to violence and abuse. And, in the last few years, children have been kept in cages on the US border with Mexico, for the crime of trying to escape violence in Central

America –just one illustration of how much discrimination on the grounds of place of birth is still widely embraced and legally enforced.

Talking of children, you might think there is excess discrimination on the grounds of *when* people were born –that you are denied too many opportunities simply because you haven't had enough birthdays. Personally, I am against twelve-year-olds being allowed to drive a car, but I'm a lot less sure about the movie restrictions, the rules against being at home (or in public) alone, or the age at which people can drink alcohol. And I wonder why American sixteen-year-olds can't vote (they can in Argentina and Brazil).

In many other countries, terrible abuses against rights are a regularity. Saudi Arabia still prescribes beheadings and crucifixion for crimes ranging from not believing in God through homosexuality to insulting the royal family. China is undertaking mass arrests and imprisonment of the Uigher minority. Many of Burma's Rohingya people have been attacked and killed. In Southern Africa in recent years, some countries have made laws against homosexuality even harsher than they already were. Women in Russia are legally banned from working in many jobs that require heavy labor, that involve dangerous working conditions, or take place underground –and those are just some of many thousands of legal restrictions worldwide that stop women working equally with men. And still 15 million girls are married before they are 18 each year.

The world's governments have all agreed that child marriage is wrong and have promised to work towards ending it, but there is still a long way to go. Similarly, we have seen that nearly all of the World's governments have signed up to international treaties and agreements that say they will respect human rights including freedom of religion and racial and gender equality, from the Universal Declaration of Human Rights to the UN Convention on the Elimination of All Forms of Discrimination Against Women. They are breaking their own commitments when they carry out human rights abuses.

How can you help speed progress towards a freer world? First off, by recognizing discrimination. I'm a non-disabled white male of

European descent married to a white woman: I am not on the receiving end of discrimination as part of daily life. But it is a daily reality for most people on the planet, and we all have to understand and learn about the kinds of discrimination we don't face. We should think about the discrimination we practice, too, however unintentionally. Ask someone if they judge people on the color of their skin, for example, and they will almost certainly say no. But that doesn't mean they *act* the same towards people regardless of race, consciously or not.

And stand up to racism, sexism, and prejudice wherever you see it -perhaps you can even start a movement. In Pakistan, Gulalai Ismail founded a group called "Aware Girls" when she was 16. The group focuses on women's empowerment, gender equality, and peace, and as well as educating and campaigning, it organizes quarterly meetings with politicians which are open to the public but provide young women in particular the platform to question and debate with leaders about the issues that affect them most.

Or you can join the National Organization for Women or set up a chapter at your school, or take part in one of the campaigns organized by the National LGBTQ Task Force. Join Black Lives Matter protests. Or join groups like Amnesty International that fight for human rights worldwide.

Discrimination is not only wrong, but also stupid. Denying people equal opportunities on the grounds of their disability, race, religion, gender, or sexual identity is bad for those discriminated against but it is also bad for those doing the discriminating. Black women have the natural talents to be as good surgeons as white men, for example. If you discriminate against them, the average quality of surgeons will be lower —because you'll replace the most talented black women with middle-talented white men. Your discrimination gets you lower quality health care. So, it is smart to be in favor of equal opportunity —and the world is a richer and healthier place in part because discrimination is declining.

116

Democracy

Members of the US Constitutional Convention: democracy limited to rich white men with wig wardrobes was still a bit better than what came before. (Source: Wikimedia).

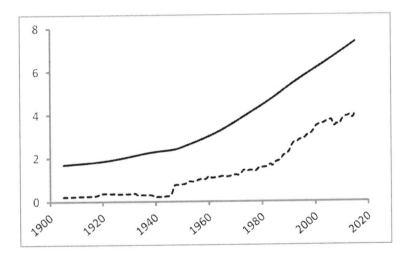

The world's total population (solid line) and the population living in a democracy (dotted line).

Between December 1788 and January 1789, Americans voted for a president for the first time. To be more accurate, *some* Americans voted for a president. The 69 members of the electoral college who chose George Washington had themselves been chosen by five state governments and six state elections involving a (more or less) popular vote. Perhaps less than 45,000 Americans actually directly got to vote for an electoral college representative out of a population closer to 3,900,000 strong. And those 45,000 (or about one percent) were hardly a representative cross section of the nation.

Adding in people who had an indirect say in the choice of Washington through their state representatives, those with the right to vote made up about one out of every ten Americans. Women and free black men were largely excluded alongside all Native Americans and slaves —and those under the age of 21. And many states only let people vote if they owned land or property. In subsequent elections, free blacks and women were increasingly denied the right to vote even as many property requirements were abandoned, extending the right to more white men.

But in 1790, even though America was far, far away from equal political rights for all, and if anything moving in the wrong direction, it was the most democratic country in the world. Today, America is considerably closer to the promise of democracy for all than it was in 1790, and much of the rest of the world has caught up.

Democracy isn't just about getting the right to mark a piece of paper or tap a screen to choose a mayor or president. You have to have a choice worth making, between candidates free to express their views who will have the power to influence government policies if they get elected. Take the election for President in Haiti in 1962 as an example of a not-exactly-democratic process: candidate Francois Duvalier won by 1,320,748 votes to zero, helped considerably by the fact he was the only candidate on the ballot paper.

And in a true democracy you should have a similar influence over the shape of government as your neighbors and fellow citizens —the same ability to vote, the same impact of that vote on the outcome.

Because democracy involves a whole system and how it functions, there is no clear dividing line between democratic and undemocratic countries, nor is it always clear which countries are more democratic than others. The extremes are obvious: no one would argue China under Chairman Mao or Russia under Stalin was a democracy. But any reckoning of which countries are democratic, or even how democratic they are, is going to be arguable.

That's important to remember, because I'm about to list a bunch of statistics about the number of democratic countries or the number of people who live in a democracy. The researchers who put those numbers together try to be consistent, at least, so that two countries with the same system should be labeled or scored the same —democratic or not. But their decisions on what counts as a country being democratic might not be the same as your decision. Some of the numbers below are based on a scoring system that puts the United States in the democracy column in 1790, for example –you might look at a voting population that was nearly all male, and nearly all white, and wonder a bit about that. So, take the numbers as at least arguably reflecting trends, but still maybe missing out a considerable amount of what really matters.

Look at more recent US history: even though by the time your grandparents began voting participation for blacks and women had been guaranteed by amendments to the constitution, there were still huge obstacles put in the way of black voters from supposed 'literacy tests' (with scores made up to exclude black applicants) through violence and intimidation. The effort to take away the vote from blacks got worse over time: across the Southern states of the US, black participation in elections fell considerably between the 1870s and the 1950s. Only thanks to protest, registration drives and the Voting Rights Act of 1965 was the process reversed. When your parents began voting in the 1990s, black participation in elections was still about ten percent lower than white participation, but by the elections in the 2000s that gap had largely closed.

Worldwide, in 1960, 245 million people still lived in a colony –a country ruled by an empire. 1,160 million people lived in a democracy and 1,615 million in dictatorships or countries with weak democratic rights. Today, pretty much no-one lives in a colony, 4,100 million live in a democracy and 3,250 million in a dictatorship or country in transition towards democracy. The share living in a democracy has gone from under four out of ten to more than half. About 29 countries were democracies in 1960. That had climbed to 41 in 1980. Today the figure is 99 countries, which is the majority of the world's total.

Into the 1970s, in most countries in the world, the legislature (like the Congress in the US) and the Chief Executive (the President in the US) weren't elected. Today, in almost every country worldwide, they are elected. Elections can be bought, opposition candidates locked up and the media told what to report, but even many of the most dictatorial governments go through the pretense of a voting process. Since the 1990s there have been a little less than seventy national elections each year worldwide compared to between 30 and 40 in the 1970s.

And the right to vote is increasingly recognized as something that belongs to all adults. Because of exclusions of people who couldn't read, or didn't pay taxes, or were women, or were the 'wrong' skin color, only twenty percent of South African adults could vote in 1950 along with one percent of Kenyans, seven percent of Nigerians, 50 percent of Brazilians and Iranians. Paraguay, Afghanistan, Iran and Switzerland all banned women from voting. Today, almost universally, every adult has the right to vote regardless of race, gender, wealth, or education.

Why has democracy spread? Richer, more educated countries tend to be more democratic, and the world has been getting richer and more educated. That said, many economists would argue that democracy helps promote economic growth and widespread education —and it could be that all three are both cause and effect of each other all at the same time.

I think another reason for its spread is that democracy is, simply, a rather powerful idea. Once you think about it, why *shouldn't* you get a say in who runs your town or your country? Certainly, it is an idea that is accepted worldwide: in opinion surveys carried out in sixty countries, big majorities of people everywhere say it is important to live in a democracy and a bit smaller majorities everywhere say that an important feature of democracy is that people choose their leaders in free elections.

That said, there's probably no such thing as a perfect democracy, and the ones we've got are certainly a long way from anyone's idea of perfection. The 700,000 voters of Washington DC don't get one senator to represent them, let alone two —despite that the District's population is considerably larger than Vermont or Wyoming (and Puerto Rico has three million people represented by zero senators). That every state gets two senators is one reason why there are 290,000 voters per senator in Wyoming compared to 19,760,000 voters per senator in California. Again, there remain considerable efforts to keep poor and minority voters from the polls including the fact that election day isn't a day off work and there are fewer polling stations in poorer parts of the country that are home to larger minority populations. Rich people have an easier time voting, getting their views reflected in laws and regulations, and getting elected: most senators and representatives in Washington are millionaires.

That's to say nothing of the government decisions that are taken for reasons that have little to do with popular opinion or the defense of rights. In the United States, seven percent of adults say they paid a bribe to a government official last year to get something —maybe paying the policeman rather than get a speeding ticket, or paying the inspector for not reporting that their house or car doesn't meet safety standards. That compares to a lot less than one percent in the UK, or three percent in France.

But it also compares to 51 percent of adults in Mexico or 69 percent in India who say they paid a bribe to a government official in the past year. And that reflects even larger challenges to democracy in many other countries. The researchers that study global democracy mostly agree the world has been moving backward in the last few years. Some big examples include Russia, India, the Philippines, and

Brazil, where dictatorial rulers are using their power to harass and disadvantage their political opponents. China has never been democratic, but in the last two years it has reduced the limited democratic rights enjoyed by citizens of the Chinese city of Hong Kong.

And we are a long way from anything close to democratic systems to respond to the global issues we face. Voting at the United Nations suffers from the same problem as the US Senate, only worse: small states like Nauru (population about 10,000) have the same number of votes as large states like India (with a population 135,000 times as large). Added to that, the country representatives who sit in the United Nations General Assembly are appointed by governments, not elected by their people. Other international organizations including the World Bank apportion votes based on country wealth —rich countries get more votes than poor ones. There isn't a single global organization which makes decisions based on the idea of equal representation of the world's people.

If you're in the target age group for this book, you can't vote in city, state, and federal elections yet. But that doesn't mean you can't take part in democracy. For a start, the last few years have demonstrated the power of protests and marches to change things for the better: not least, they encourage more people who *can* vote to go to the polls. You can volunteer on political campaigns and write letters to your representatives. And if you want to vote sooner, join the campaign at Vote16USA.org. If you are interested in global democracy, take part in a model United Nations, or join the United Nations Association.

Even if you managed to live under a rock wearing headphones and glued solely to Disney Plus since your birth, you'll know that a lot of people in America have been concerned about the status of democracy in this country over the past ten years –that Congress isn't working, that the Presidency is in crisis. There is even more reason to worry in many faltering democracies around the world. But we are still at least near the historic high point of global democratic rights. The cliché is that democracy is the worst form of government apart from all the others, and it is true. So, hopefully, we'll see progress resume soon. Global trends towards higher education, less discrimination and greater wealth are reasons to think it will –but protesting and campaigning help, too.

Happiness and Depression

Peasants dancing at a wedding in 1607. Apparently, it was possible to be happy even before indoor plumbing and YouTube cat videos (Source: Wikimedia).

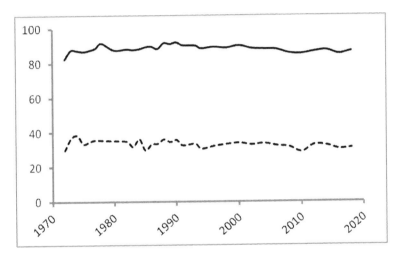

The dotted line is the proportion of Americans who say they are very happy. The solid line adds in those who say they are (just) happy.

In 1824, the English poet Samuel Taylor Coleridge suggested what he thought about the role of money in making for a happy family. "Show me one couple unhappy merely on account of their limited circumstances," he said, "and I will show you ten who are wretched from other causes." On the one hand, that sounds completely reasonable – that money is no guarantee of happiness is surely one of the most repeated ideas in the self-help industry. But it is still odd: Coleridge was writing at a time when the average person in Britain lived on an income about one twentieth that of the average American today. Britain's wealth in 1824 compares to some of the very poorest countries in the world in 2020. And yet Coleridge wasn't the first person to suggest lack of money was a minor cause of misery –it was a clichéd idea even then.

Forget money: how can it be that *anyone* was *ever* happy at a time when even the richest families would have expected some of their children to die before they turned five, where no-one had any electronics and only a tiny minority had a single book, when most houses were windowless hovels, when violence was everywhere and freedoms routinely crushed?

And yet, from what we know of the past, not everyone was constantly depressed: people smile in paintings; books describe contented men and women; being miserable was worthy of comment and concern. That makes happiness and depression different from most of the things we've talked about up to now. There *may* be a global trend to greater reported happiness, but it is a *lot* less clear than some of the other trends we've seen, which raises questions as to why, and what (if anything) we can do about it.

In the United States, pollsters started asking people if "taking your life as a whole, do you consider yourself unhappy, somewhat happy, or very happy" around 1947, when your grandparents were young. They've kept on asking, and while the number of people who say they are happy has wiggled up and down, it isn't too much different from what it was seventy years ago. We saw in the introduction that most people report they are content, but the proportions haven't shifted. If you ask people worldwide "are you happy?" about four out of five say yes, far higher than most people would guess. But, at best, that is a bit higher than in the past (the surveys don't go back very far in most countries).

You'd be right to wonder about using survey responses to the question 'are you happy' to make strong global statements about levels of contentment. There are lots of good reasons to be concerned: do people mean the same when they answer 'somewhat happy' in Finland as when they answer 'somewhat happy' in China? Do people tell the truth or answer what they think pollsters want to hear? That said, these survey answers match the answers that friends say they would give about the person being asked, and tests suggest people do mean close to the same thing when they answer 'somewhat happy' across time and across countries.

The idea of limited progress in happiness that comes across in polls is also confirmed by looking at those who appear most unhappy. The rate of suicide in the United States is a little higher than it was in the 1950s and 1980s, and it has climbed by about a third since 2000. Worldwide, suicide kills twice the number of people who die in murders. Suicide rates are climbing in some countries and falling in others, with perhaps a small overall decline since 1990.

About seven percent of all US adults –over 17 million people– had what the National Institute of Mental Health called a major depressive episode in 2017. That is two weeks or more when a person experienced a depressed mood or loss of interest in daily activities, and suffered symptoms including problems with sleep, eating, energy, concentration, or loss of self-worth.

And you know that anxiety and depression affect people young and old alike. About thirteen percent of people age twelve to seventeen suffer one or more depressive episodes in a year. The global data on depression is too patchy to make any strong statements about trends: a sign of how the world pays far too little attention to mental health.

So, why isn't everyone living in a state of ecstasy about their long lives, the indoor plumbing, the ability to see things after dark, the safer jobs and all the rest? Maybe one reason is biology: it would be a bit of a design flaw in humans if being happy took a level of wealth that pretty much no-one had for ninety nine percent of the time people have been on the planet. On the other hand, it would be extremely odd if fewer kids dying, fewer people hungry and fewer people being beaten up or killed wasn't a cause of a bit more contentment.

It wasn't that people didn't care about death or quality of life in the past: writers through history have mourned the loss of the young, for example. But people had coping mechanisms. One response to frequent death was fatalism, the sense that there was nothing that could be done, that the deaths were inevitable. The idea it was "God's will" provided comfort, as did the idea an afterlife of ease awaited the moral and upstanding sufferer after death. And regarding access to physical stuff like books, or technologies like telephones, it is hard to resent not having what no-one has.

Not knowing what you are missing is one reason why when you ask people "how much money would it take to make you rich," the answer they give is relative to what they know. Occasionally, people on Twitter and Facebook will ridicule an article written by someone (usually living in New York) who says they are "struggling to get by" on an income of a few hundred thousand dollars a year. What the somewhat socially unaware author is saying in those articles is closer to "I can't afford the quality of life my friends and neighbors have on less than half a million a year."

At the other end of the scale, what counts as poverty depends a lot on how rich a country is. So, the US has an income per person of about $138 a day and the official poverty line is set at about $22 a day. Russia has an average income per person of $69 and the poverty line is $8 a day. Malawi has an average income of a little less than $3 a day and poverty line of $1.27.

Within the US, richer people do tend to be a bit happier than poorer people. And across the world, the average person is a bit happier in a rich country than they are in a poor one. Losing an arm or a leg can dent happiness—at least for a bit. Middle age is associated with a bit of a happiness dip. And having kids doesn't seem to have much impact at all in how happy parents report themselves.

Just in case this makes you feel under-appreciated, one explanation is that while the actual kid makes parents feel happier, the financial stress associated with buying all the stuff the kid needs – backpacks, food, Animal Crossing games– makes parents a bit less happy. Given the US Department of Agriculture reckons it costs $233,610 to raise a child to the age of 17, think of yourself as having the same impact on your parent's or guardian's happiness as a quarter of a million dollars dropped in their lap.

But to be honest, I'd argue it isn't really about the money. I think having a child ties some of the parent's happiness to the kid's: when the kid is happy, the parents are happy, when the kid is sad, the parents are sad. Overall, if the average kid is as happy as the average parent, they're going to have little impact on average parental happiness. Which just goes to show there is more to life than how happy people say they are, because I'd value my children at a lot more than $233,610 each and I *know* they make my life more meaningful in ways uncountable and immeasurable (as well as more frustrating, aggravating, scary and annoying, of course –but mainly the good stuff).

Add together money, if people are married or have children, if you are in good or bad health, age, education —all of it seems to explain only a rather small part of why some people say they are happy, and others say they aren't. A few things are more closely related: being unemployed can severely decrease reported happiness, while happy people have more friends. And having more stuff matters less to happiness scores than having new experiences. Maybe all of that's a sign that feeling socially connected and socially useful is the secret to contentment, and it is a reason to believe the practical gap between the idea of leading a good life and the desire to lead a happy life is not all that big.

But the fact that how you are doing compared to how you think you could be doing that seems to matter more to happiness than how you are doing compared to how people have done in the past suggests the world could continue to get healthier, richer, better educated and less prone to violence, and there would still be lots of people who say they are unhappy. We still need coping mechanisms to deal with tragedy, deprivation and suffering even if they are relatively less common than in the past.

And there would continue to be people who are depressed or feel suicidal as well. In most countries, old people are more likely to take their own life than the young, and an aging population might be one reason for climbing suicide rates in the US. The most common illness associated with suicide is depression, but other mental disorders can also bring on suicidal acts. Once again, that all suggests how far we need to go as a country and a planet in responding to the problem of mental health.

It turns out that the best thing you can do for the happiness of others may be the best thing you can do for your own happiness –engage with people, form generous friendships, live a life with the purpose of making the world around you a better place.

If you are feeling anxious, depressed, or suicidal, the most important step to deal with the problem at any age is to tell someone who can help. Doctors and medicines can really make a difference to mental health, just as with any other illness, and, just as with any other illness, it isn't your fault.

Again, telling someone who can help is the most important thing you can do if you see friends or a family member who is acting withdrawn or depressed, or talking about hurting themselves. You can reach out to school counsellors or an adult you feel comfortable talking to. In the US, the national suicide prevention lifeline is 1-800-273-8255, and it provides free, completely confidential support.

So, the good news is the world is a reasonably happy place overall. The bad news is it doesn't seem to be rapidly getting happier in the way it is getting rapidly healthier and richer. Nonetheless, the evidence suggests that being open and generous to other people is probably good for your happiness as well as theirs. As a rule, and for all the horrors of social media trolling and cyber-bullying, we seem to be getting a bit better at that over time. We'd be doing even better if the world paid more attention to the illness of depression – hopefully, your generation will be more aware of the illness, more willing to talk about it, and better able to respond to it.

The Environment

The Kaburas' source of cooking, lighting and heating —and the world's most urgent pollution challenge (Gapminder/ Dollar Street).

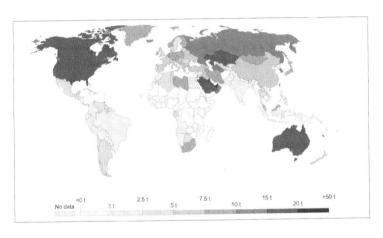

Carbone dioxide pollution per person per year in tons (darker is more pollution): the US doesn't look so good (Source: Our World in Data).

In December 1952, a cold snap hit London —Britain's capital city. For four days, the freeze was combined with windless conditions. People burned a lot of coal in their houses to keep warm, and power plants near the center of the city in Battersea and Bankside burned more coal as well, to make electricity for space heaters. The yellow-black soot from chimneys was trapped in the still, foggy air, where it combined with diesel exhaust from busses and more coal exhaust from steam trains. The 'smog' created by all this pollution was so thick, people could only see for a few feet. Ambulances stopped running for fear of accidents and cinemas closed because people couldn't see the screens.

But the biggest effect was on people's breathing. The pollution of smoke —small dust particles, sulfuric acid, and hydrochloric acid— ate into the lungs of exposed Londoners. As many as 12,000 people died because of the Great Smog of London, mostly children and the elderly.

Thanks to cleaner fuels for heating and better engines for transport, London doesn't suffer smogs anymore, and the buildings are no longer coated with a layer of black soot. And that's a sign we can make progress against environmental challenges if we make the effort.

American cities don't suffer from deadly smogs like they used to, either. In 1974, around when your parents were born, a Stage Three Smog Alert was issued for Upland in Los Angeles, and California governor Ronald Reagan told the city's residents to limit all unnecessary travel. Thankfully, that was America's last Stage Three Alert, as smog got better because of regulations on pollution. But in 1990, there were still 42 Stage One Alerts in the city –where air pollution was bad enough that children and the elderly were advised to stay indoors if they could. 2000 was the first year that the city saw no Stage One alerts.

Sadly, recent wildfires in the states have given California residents a taste of what life used to be like. But still, thanks to cleaner air in the United States, the number of people who die because of air pollution has halved since 1990. Sulfur dioxide emissions (which, mixed with water, produce an acid) are at one tenth their level of 1970, emissions of particulates (tiny grains of soot that can coat the lungs) at one fifth the level and emissions of nitrogen oxides (again, acidic in water) are at less than half the level of 1970.

And it is not just the US that has seen recent progress. In 1940, the world produced 51 million tonnes of sulfur dioxide. By 1960, that had almost doubled, and in 1980 emissions reached 151 million tonnes. The good news is that this was the peak. By 2010, the world was back below 100 million tonnes. Worldwide, as in America, deaths from air pollution have fallen by almost one half since 1990.

Air pollution has become less of a problem because new technologies have made heating, cooking and cars far cleaner, while government regulation has helped speed the introduction of those technologies and ensured power plants and industries don't belch dirty smoke. The combination has meant people can still drive, cook, and heat and cool their houses while they also enjoy relatively clean air.

But still about 4,200,000 people worldwide die each year from outdoor air pollution and a further 3,800,000 people die from the smoke and gasses produced in their houses from cooking, heating, and lighting using dirty fuels like dung, coal or wood (like the Kabura family in Burundi does). That makes local air pollution the most urgent environmental issue we face worldwide.

In the recent past, *global* atmospheric pollution has become an increasing concern. As your parents reached school age, a new threat emerged. Ozone high up in the atmosphere absorbs ultraviolet light —the part of the sun's rays that causes sun tans but also burns and skin cancer. In the 1980s, scientists found that ozone levels had dropped dramatically over the Antarctic, with the risk that the ozone hole could expand to cover the rest of the planet. A major cause of the ozone hole was chlorofluorocarbons —chemicals used to help refrigerators work and to power spray bottles, but which had a side effect of destroying ozone when they were released into the air.

In 1987, the world's countries came together to sign the Montreal Protocol, that limited global production of chlorofluorocarbons. The ozone hole began to shrink shortly after. The global effort to save the ozone layer will prevent 280 million cases of skin cancer and 1,500,000 deaths in the United States alone up to 2100.

Chlorofluorocarbons are a greenhouse gas – they cause climate change. Sadly, so are methane and carbon dioxide, and our global output of those gasses continues to climb. The amount of carbon dioxide the world creates per dollar of goods and services we produce has been going down since the 1950s, but because we're producing a lot more goods and services, we are still producing more carbon dioxide. The world is already about one degree centigrade warmer than it was 100 years ago as a result.

We need to make much more rapid progress in making stuff without making greenhouse gasses. If we don't, the world's climate will be around two or three degrees warmer still by the time you are entering your 90s. Two degrees centigrade is the difference between average temperatures in Detroit, Michigan and Indianapolis, Indiana. That may not sound like much, but that's the average worldwide –temperatures will rise more in some of the world's hottest places, which are also some of the world's poorest places, which can least afford air conditioning and other ways of making hotter temperatures less of a problem. And two to three degrees is a best estimate: things could be better, but they could be considerably worse. Regardless, if your generation doesn't help change course, the effects that will be felt by your children and grandchildren in the 22nd Century will be even bigger.

And because of melting glaciers and ice sheets, the sea may be 50 centimeters (more than a foot and a half) higher on average by the time you are approaching 90 years old. Again, that's an average –it will be higher in some places, especially during storms. And, again, it's an estimate: sea rise might be more rapid if some big glaciers collapse into the ocean faster than we expect. That means more people who live near coasts will risk more flooding than they do today. Once again, the poorest people in tropical areas will be affected the most, because they will be least able to afford sea walls and other defenses against storms.

As the world got richer, the risk of dying from climate-related disasters like floods, hurricanes, tsunamis, and heat waves in particular has fallen fivefold since the 1980s. But as those disasters get more likely and more intense, poor countries will need more resources to respond. And if we don't act, the global economic cost of climate change will be in the trillions of dollars —far more than the cost of introducing clean power or other technologies to slow climate change.

We face a lot of environmental challenges beyond air pollution and climate change: the rate of plant and animal extinctions has sped up to perhaps 100 times the frequency of two centuries ago (the good news: that still suggests a rate of extinction of about two species a year, so we are still a long way from a 'mass extinction event' like the one that killed off the last dinosaurs). A huge number of larger animal species that haven't gone extinct have seen population declines of sixty percent or more in the last five decades. Insects, too, have seen collapsing populations.

In addition, we've seen: 'dead zones' in the ocean linked to acidification from carbon dioxide in the atmosphere and farm fertilizers washing off fields; tropical deforestation; plastics pollution; and water shortages. But the fact that we have already reversed course on several environmental problems from local air pollution through bald eagle endangerment through acid rain to ozone depletion should give us hope we can fix these problems too.

With climate as well as with other pollution and issues like deforestation, the answer is to reduce our 'environmental footprint': to use less resources and land to produce goods and services. The story of how tomato production has changed since your grandparents were young shows we can do that. In 1961, the average farm in the United States produced 25 tonnes of tomatoes per hectare. A big tomato weighs about 100 grams, a tonne is 1,000 kilograms, so that is about 250,000 tomatoes. Meanwhile, a hectare is about the size of a sports field. So, farms grew a quarter of a million tomatoes per sports field.

Today the average tomato farm produces one million tomatoes in each sports field. In India, the average tomato farm still only produces 250,000 tomatoes per hectare, but that's still more than two and a half times what Indian farm produced back in 1961. Again, between the 1860s and the1940s, the average farm in the United States produced two tonnes of corn per acre. In the 1970s that reached six tonnes and in recent years over ten tonnes. That production isn't always sustainable: it can leach soils of nutrients while simultaneously flooding rivers with excess fertilizer. Sometimes it involves taking more water out of local sources than is sustainable. But it's still a start.

And it is good news, because that we can reduce our environmental footprint means the World doesn't have to get a lot poorer to save the climate or reduce species loss, it 'only' has to get even more efficient at turning land, resources and carbon emissions into quality of life.

Look at energy production: renewable sources like solar panels and wind farms don't produce carbon dioxide, smoke, nitrous oxides or sulfur, so they help with both local and global pollution issues. And they are getting cheaper: the cost of a solar power module is less than one hundredth of what it was in 1980, for example. Most countries can't (yet) get most of their energy from renewable sources, but we are moving in that direction.

Again, we can see that using less carbon is possible at a high quality of life by looking across countries: the United States emits 16.5 tonnes of carbon dioxide per person each year —doing things like driving cars, producing electricity, and making cement. But Switzerland, where the average resident is a little richer than in the US, emits only 4.7 tonnes of carbon dioxide per person each year. Swiss people eat about half as much meat per year as the average American, they drive less, they live in smaller houses, and make a bunch of other decisions as a country that mean a high quality of life does less harm to the climate.

What makes responding to environmental challenges complex is the number of people involved. Think about peeing in the pool. If you did it alone, most of the pool still wouldn't be pee. In fact, the pool would be about 7,500,000 parts *not* urine for every part that is urine. Once it had spread around a bit, nobody would notice. But then if a bunch of other people urinate in the pool, every one of them going 'well, it doesn't matter if I pee in the pool, it will still be mostly not pee...' suddenly everyone's eyes start stinging from the mixed chlorine and urine.

If you don't pee in the pool, that's a start, but unless other people don't pee in the pool either, your eyes will still sting if you forget your swimming goggles. So, if you are going to make sure the pool doesn't sting your eyes —or anyone else's eyes—

you've got to be part of a way to stop everyone doing it. To solve the problem, you have to work together.

Economists call this type of problem a 'commons issue,' and dealing with them using taxes and regulations is a big part of the reason the world has got better over time. For problems like climate change and the ozone hole, the pool we are talking about is the planet's atmosphere —everyone worldwide can pee in it, so everyone worldwide needs to be part of the solution. Global treaties like those agreed at a series of UN conferences from Kyoto to Paris that commit countries to reduce their carbon dioxide emissions have had some effect, but they need to be much stronger and countries should commit to faster reductions.

At the same time, it is important to remember that it is richer people and countries who use more electricity, who travel more, and who can heat and cool their (larger) houses. We've seen many of the world's poorest people don't have electricity at all, they don't own cars and they burn dung and wood for cooking and heating. Giving those people access to electricity and natural gas will reduce their risk of dying from air pollution and hugely improve their quality of life. And even if they get a bit richer, because they are still going to be relatively poor, and spend less on everything including fuel, people in poor countries will still account for the fraction of the greenhouse gas emissions that the world's richer people –including you and me—are already responsible for.

Given the world's poorest people will suffer some of the most from climate change, and they are some of the least responsible for climate change occurring, they shouldn't be forced to pay for fixing the problem as well. So, rich countries should lead on global cooperation to fix the climate: they should make it more expensive to release greenhouse gasses in their countries by taxing those who pollute, and they should make it cheaper for everybody worldwide to avoid producing greenhouse gasses in the first place by developing new technologies for power, transport, construction and agriculture that don't belch carbon dioxide or methane. The more that rich country governments like the United States fund research into cleaner energy technologies and regulate so that they are introduced here, the easier the transition to low-carbon economic growth will be for poorer countries in the future.

Similarly, with biodiversity, one factor in so many different species being concentrated in poorer countries worldwide –and especially big species like rhinos known as 'megafauna'—is that the big wild species have died out faster in more populated, richer areas of the world. If we want poor countries to preserve large areas for big animals, we should pay them.

International agreements coupled with support to developing countries can turn around species loss. In 1913, there were about 10 million elephants in Africa. That number fell to 286,000 in 1995. The good news is that it has climbed above 40,000 since then. That's thanks in part to an international ban on the sale of the ivory made from elephant tusks. Or look at international agreements against whaling: between 1900 and 1910, about 52,000 whales were caught and killed worldwide for food and oil. By the 1960s that had climbed to 703,000 whales. But countries started instituting whaling bans in the 1970s and in the last decade fewer than 10,000 whales were killed. (For all of that, some species are on the brink of extinction: there were about 340,000 blue whales worldwide in 1890, now there are less than 5,000.)

What can you do to help the global environment? Eating less meat is one step, because animals belch methane, a powerful greenhouse gas, and because meat takes a lot more land and energy to produce than grains, fruit and vegetables.

Probably your other biggest contribution to climate change is travel. So, when you can, try to walk or take the bus or subway rather than asking your parents for a ride. Buying less stuff and re-using things can also help.

But to get the world as a whole onto a more sustainable path, we need regulations and new technologies, so go out there and protest on Earth Day and tell governments to work together to find solutions.

You'll know the story of the lone student who stood outside the Swedish parliament in August 2018 demanding action on climate. Greta Thunberg's protest, shared worldwide on Twitter and Instagram, sparked a movement that expanded to 200 countries. On 20 September 2019, 4 million young people in 4,000 cities in 167 countries participated in a school strike for climate. Thunberg admonished leaders gathered at the UN: "You come to us young people for hope. How dare you. You have stolen my dreams and my childhood with your empty words."

That was 27 years after 12-year-old Severn Cullis-Suzuki told the United Nations Earth Summit in Rio "I'm only a child and I don't have all the solutions, but I want you to realize, neither do you." Given how much climate and biodiversity are issues that have generational effects, adults should be more willing to listen to children when they talk about the subject.

Several global justice groups including Oxfam work on climate and the environment as part of their mission –join them. If you are concerned about biodiversity and extinction, the World Wildlife Fund tries to conserve nature and reduce the most pressing threats to diversity.

The environment, alongside global happiness, isn't like most of the other topics covered in this book. For health, education, housing, wealth, violence and rights, the overall global trends are strongly positive. For the environment, it depends what you look at: in some cases, we're reversing past losses (forests outside the tropics, local air pollution) in other cases things are still getting worse (tropical forests, greenhouse gas emissions, species loss). But both broader global progress and the progress we've seen around some of the deadliest environmental issues shows we have the capacity to fix big problems. Add to that we know the solutions to the climate challenge and the fact that young people are more environmentally aware than any previous generation, and there are lots of reasons for hope – if your generation keeps on leading the demand for change.

The Future?

In about seven billion years, the sun will expand enough that Earth will be vaporized. If you plan to be around then, you should have a backup planet ready (Source: Wikimedia)

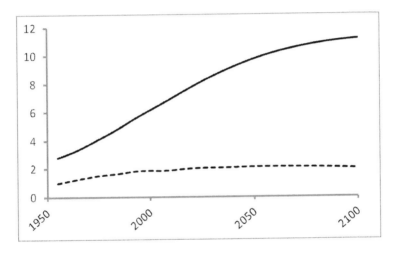

World population to 2100 in billions. The dotted line is the population under age fifteen. In a century the planet will be a bit more crowded and a lot older.

In 1930, the Economist John Maynard Keynes wrote an essay about ""Economic Possibilities for our Grandchildren." He was thinking about what the world would look like in a century –pretty much around now.

Keynes was writing at the start of the Great Depression, a decade of high unemployment and growing poverty in the US and worldwide. "We are suffering just now from a bad attack of economic pessimism," he wrote. "It is common to hear people say that the epoch of enormous economic progress ... is over; that the rapid improvement in the standard of life is now going to slow down..."

Keynes was more confident, predicting "the standard of life in progressive countries one hundred years hence will be between four and eight times as high as it is." Income is only one partial measure of "the standard of life," but it suggests Keynes was about right: average incomes in the US and Keynes' home country of Britain are about five or six times higher than they were in 1930.

Keynes also predicted one half of what we've seen was a massive change in the nature of work: "in our own lifetimes," he suggested, "we may be able to perform all the operations of agriculture, mining, and manufacture with a quarter of the human effort to which we have been accustomed."

But what he got wrong was what all of this meant in terms of how people spent their time. Keynes predicted that if fewer people were needed to do agriculture, mining, and manufacturing, that meant there would be less work to do overall. He said we'd enter "the age of leisure and of abundance," where the worry would be how people would occupy all of their free time in a world where no-one would work more than fifteen hours a week.

We've seen Keynes was off base. People found a whole assortment of new jobs to do, and the work week most places remains stubbornly at forty hours. And people have certainly found things they want to buy with their money, including a number of technologies undreamed of in Keynes' time.

What are the possibilities for you and your grandchildren at the start of the Twenty Second Century (if you have children, and if they have children)? Keynes' record suggests it is easier to predict a pattern of continued economic advance than what it might mean. And a big point of this book is 'what it might mean' is up to your generation —and the one that follows it. But some things are probably reasonably safe to predict.

Today, about one in every five people on the planet are under the age of twelve and fewer than one in ten are over 65 years old. By 2100, when you'll (probably) be approaching the end of your life, the United Nations predicts it will be closer to one in ten who are pre-teens and almost a quarter who will be 65-plus. There will be a lot of company at the retirement home. Of course, depending on how much progress we make against diseases of the old, you might not be in a retirement home.

There will be a few more people around, too —the World's population is predicted to top out at around 11 billion around 2100. And they'll be increasingly packed into cities —rural areas are already emptying out worldwide. But even if you're closer to more people, you'll be closely related to fewer of them. If you have kids —and that is less likely than it was— you will probably have fewer kids than your grandparents did, and that will mean you'll probably have fewer grandchildren, too.

If you are worried about being lonely, one thing that might provide comfort is that although your family will have a wealthier, healthier choice of places to live in the world than ever before, if the trends of the last forty years continue, on average they'll be living even closer to you than you do to your grandparents. Americans are moving less across state lines than they used to –in the 1980s about six in every 1,000 Americans moved to a new state each year, that's down closer to four per 1,000 today. At the same time, a *few* more Americans are making their lives abroad: about one percent of people born in the US now live in another country. But, overall, richer countries see lower migration, so that if the world keeps on getting wealthier, more people may travel to other countries for holidays but stay near to where they were born for the rest of their lives.

How much that changes depends in part on what happens to borders –how free people will be to move around the world if they want to. Aging countries might be one reason to think it will get easier to move. The proportion of those over 65 who are in work has been going up the last twenty years in the US, but it is still well below the rate in the 1970s or before that. So, whether you are working as 2100 approaches probably depends on how well you and the government save for retirement and how much you enjoy your job.

But countries where everyone wants to retire will need other people to do the work that needs to get done. The part of the world that will still have a younger population with workers to spare will be Africa. Maybe alongside continued global peace (that I hope will follow from greater wealth and stronger connections) that will be a force for more people moving from poor to rich places.

Even without much more movement, America will be majority minority country some time before 2050 –non-Latino whites will be the minority of the population. Quite possibly by 2100 what people consider a 'minority group' will have changed and, given the trend toward inter-racial marriages, racism and ethnicity will be increasingly blurred.

The weather will be warmer –even if we drastically speed up our response to climate change in the next few years. And if we don't, there will be a lot more wildfires, more coastal flooding, more hurricanes, and more heat waves. Nearly all of the world's coral reefs will die off, extinguishing one of the most fascinating and beautiful natural wonders. Rates of animal extinction will continue to rise.

Either way, we might face natural resource shortages, but they may well not be the resources we worry about today. In the 1900s we worried about running out of guano –bird poop—because it was a vital ingredient of fertilizers for crops. We don't anymore, because we invented a process to make artificial fertilizer. In the 1980s, we worried about running out of oil –now we worry about having too much for the planet's own good. Perhaps we will be worrying about running out of soap bark tree extract, used to make vaccines, or helium (which we're busy blowing into balloons without really knowing how to find more). Hopefully, we'll create technologies to respond –or better regulate the stocks we have.

We will probably continue the global trend towards using less land for agriculture, leaving more space for wildlands and forests. One thing behind that might be a growing trend to vegetarianism, sped along by improvements in fake meat. And perhaps that will foster a growing movement for animal rights as traditional forms of discrimination against humans continue to whither worldwide.

Looking at global government, it may be well more than a century before everyone on the planet gets to vote for world president (if they ever do), but that doesn't mean we won't be drawn into even closer cooperation. We often miss how much that has happened already because it is behind the scenes, but look at travel for an example. The reason flying across the world in an airplane is pretty much the safest way to move is in large part because of a whole load of international agreements about how planes are built, crewed and operated that cover everything from runway signs and how pilots talk to air traffic controllers to fuel standards and seat belt requirements.

Again, international trade got a whole lot simpler when everyone pretty much agreed most stuff was going to be traded inside of metal containers that measured 8 feet wide and 8.5 feet high (that made it much easier and quicker to load and stack cargo on ships). And on the subject of feet, measurement has got a lot more straightforward for the entire world outside the US, Burma and Liberia, because they've all agreed to use metric system –meters *instead* of feet. One day, perhaps, the holdouts will swap over.

We have international agreements on health, what boats can do at sea, how banks can borrow and lend. And that kind of cooperation is going to keep on growing because it makes sense: it makes it easier for all of us to talk, to trade, to move and to preserve the global climate and biodiversity. Hopefully, more of the global systems that support that cooperation will become democratic, so that even if you don't get to vote for world president, maybe your elected representative gets to vote in turn for head of the World Trade Organization, for example.

When it comes to broader quality of life, sometimes we talk as if people are the problem — they're poor, they pollute, they fight and argue.

People aren't perfect, but they aren't the problem, they're *us*. And if you look over the millennia, having more people around has helped make things better.

Indeed, if you were to look at the history of the planet over the past few thousand years, from the first civilizations to today, in some ways it looks remarkably predictable. The number of people has grown over time, and the speed at which it has grown has increased: it took about a thousand years to double the population between 2000 BCE and 10000 BCE, it took fifty years to more than double the world population between1970 CE and 2020 CE. The same speeding up is true of income growth: it took from 1000 BCE to 1870 to double average global incomes, while in the 150 years since then the average global income has climbed eleven-fold. If that long term trend to more rapid growth was to continue, well before 2100 we'd all be multi-billionaires but squeezed to death by the pressure of our trillions of neighbors.

It won't, of course —already population growth has slowed, and income growth hasn't gone stratospheric. But that people create progress is reason to believe that the quality of life will continue to improve. Extreme ($1.90 a day) poverty will be a thing of the past. And hopefully everyone worldwide will be living above the current US poverty line well before 2100.

But that won't necessarily make everyone content. You probably won't be much happier than you say you are now —that's for several reasons: as we've seen how happy you are doesn't change much over life, but it does tend to dip downward towards middle age, and more money or health doesn't buy you too much more. There will always be something wrong, and always something to strive for —although hopefully much more of the world will have access to high quality medical care to deal with anxiety and depression. There will doubtless be a whole range of new health technologies, as well as technologies of work and play, that would simply stun a time traveler from 2020.

There is some risk of terrible outcomes: nuclear Armageddon, bioterror or a pandemic far worse than Covid-19. Any dinosaur fan knows the risks that an asteroid can present to life on Earth and it doesn't take too many science fiction novels to understand that rogue robots could pose a threat.

But global cooperation is possible –rules on weapons research, agreements to destroy nuclear weapons, cooperation on asteroid surveying and response, agreements on regulation of artificial intelligence. Hopefully, in a more peaceful, more connected, and more democratic world, getting to those agreements will be a bit more straightforward.

Looking further forward, and if your generation fixes the problem of climate change and future generations avoid a world war, we'll probably go through another ice age in a few tens of thousands of years. In 250 million years, all the continents might have joined together again, just as they were 300 million years ago. (On the plus side, we'll all be closer together, the bad news is that there'll be less space on the beach for each of us.)

Sometime more than a billion years off, the Earth might start tilting in a different direction and about the same time the sun will heat up, which could cause the oceans to evaporate (Mars will be getting warmer too, perhaps we will all move). Even if any earthbound descendants survive all of that, they're really unlikely to last beyond around the seven billion year mark, when the Sun will have expanded so much, the Earth will have been vaporized. But that is some time off, more of an issue for your great-great-great-great- (add 200 million greats) grandchildren than for you.

The changes in global quality of life just since your grandparents were born have been incredible, and they build on accelerating progress going back a century and more before that. The world was radically different in 1950 than in 1850, it is radically different today than it was in 1950. Not all of that difference is good, but a lot of it is. And there's no good reason to think we're at a precipice for progress. In all likelihood, and despite the last few years of stutters in health and democracy, the world will get even better over the next few decades. But, again, that's increasingly up to you.

Conclusion: The Greatest Generation

A member of the generation that's the Greatest of All Time reads to a goat (Source: National Park Service)

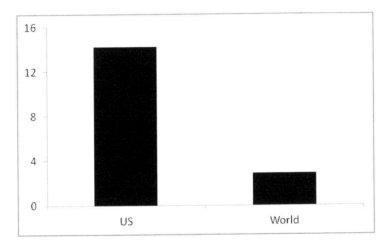

Jeff Bezos, the world's richest man, is worth about $190 billion. That's about the same amount of money as the US government spends every fourteen days and the world's governments together spend every three days.

Hans Rosling was a Swedish doctor who spent his life working on global health. He studied medicine in Bangalore, India, worked in a district clinic in Mozambique and fought an outbreak of Ebola in Liberia. He also gave several entertaining talks on global progress that you can watch online. One of the things Dr. Rosling was most interested in was how much people knew about progress, so he put together a multiple-choice test with questions like "what is world life expectancy?" "what proportion of the world can read?" and "what has happened to world poverty over the past twenty years?"

When he gave the test, the results were usually awful. On most questions, test takers would have done much better if they guessed at random. As Rosling said, chimpanzees would score better than people. That's because we think we know the world is trending towards horrible and so we consistently choose answers like 'poverty is going up' when the right answer is 'poverty is going down.'

About two thirds of America think the crime rate is going up. It is going down. Two thirds of Americans think global poverty has doubled over the past twenty years —on one common measure it has halved. Most people think child deaths have risen worldwide —they have declined at the fastest rate ever.

One reason things getting better isn't front page news and many people take some persuading to accept that it's true is that a lot of the progress we've talked about in this book is about bad things not happening to people: not needing to use a field as their toilet, not getting sick, not fighting, not being locked up for driving a car because you are a woman.

And bad things not happening is not exciting to read or hear about (thanks for sticking with it). Nobody's going to put 'some bad stuff didn't happen today' as the lead story in the newspaper. That's why if you look at deaths covered in newspapers, about half of all stories are about people dying are about murder or terrorism. Murder and terrorism account for less than one out of every 100 deaths in the US. But they are more exciting to read about.

Still, nothing happening is great if the other choice is bad things happening. You'd rather be healthy than sick. You'd rather be left alone than bullied or arrested. Bad things not happening makes space for good stuff to happen.

So –even though it is an annoying line– count your blessings and think of everything you should be thankful for. Despite all of the challenges and problems and discomforts and disappointments you face, you are still incredibly lucky to have been born in the last few years rather than thirty or a hundred years ago, and born in the United States rather than in Haiti or the Democratic Republic of the Congo. You have won the birth lottery. You are in the right place at the right time.

Even better: one of the reasons it is the best time to be alive in the United States is that the rest of the world is getting better, too: when people in India are healthier, Americans are less likely to get sick. When people in China have a stronger economy, that makes Americans richer. When people in Liberia or Libya don't fight wars, that makes America safer. That the rest of the world is catching up to America's quality of life is good for Americans and great for them.

And one of the reasons to be hopeful about the future is that positive changes reinforce each other. Healthy people have an easier time learning and working. People who have gone to school longer are healthier and make more money. Money helps pay for healthcare and education. War and violence are less common in rich, healthy countries where everyone has gone to school. And less war and violence both saves lives and makes people secure so they can go to school and work. If we can keep this cycle of progress moving forward, America and the world will keep on improving.

That is why even though two thirds of adult Americans think their kids –you– will be worse off than they are, I think they are wrong.

The picture of progress in the United States over the past few years is considerably more mixed than the picture regarding global progress. The country has seen rising inequality, stagnating, or declining incomes for many, slow progress against discrimination, rising costs for things that are increasingly important to the prospects for a good life including education, four years of immense political upheaval –all that before Covid-19. Martin

Luther King said that "the arc of the moral universe is long, but it bends toward justice." For the last few years, it certainly feels to me like we've been lagging the arc.

But the good news is that these problems have solutions: we know how to make America a more equal union, with more liberty and greater justice for all. Again, if there are solutions, it is our fault if we don't make things better. We need to get back to bending that arc: it won't bend itself.

Surveys suggest that while young Americans are more concerned about climate change than older people, they're also more optimistic about what quality of life is likely to be like in thirty years. I think they are right on both counts. We have serious national and global problems to deal with, but the future looks bright.

Slowly, generation by generation, in fits and starts, our powers of creativity, cooperation and compassion are winning out over ignorance and selfishness to create a better world —and there is no reason at all to think that process permanently stopped sometime in the 2010s.

But progress creates new responsibilities. If you simply can't help someone or don't know they need help, it isn't your fault if you don't help them. Seventy years ago — when your grandparents were kids— there weren't many antibiotics to kill bacteria. There weren't a lot of the vaccines we have now. If someone got sick with polio, there was only so much you could do for them. Maybe they would die, but nobody could say it was anyone's fault.

Now, we have both knowledge of the problem combined with knowledge of how to fix it. There are lots of antibiotics, and many cost just cents a pill. If someone dies from polio, it is everyone's fault. Together, we can easily afford to get the polio vaccine to everyone who needs it. If we don't, we've done something wrong. It isn't your fault or my fault, but it is *our* fault. We –you—need to fix that.

It may seem impossible to make things better for the hundreds of millions who lack fresh water or the billions who will suffer from a warmer climate but there are three important things to remember: first, each one of those hundreds of millions is a person. They have a name and a family and dreams and fears, they have a favorite game and a food they hate just like you. So, if you can help just a few of those people get fresh water or find a safe place to live, or be part of a project that gets millions fresh water or a safe place to live, you have done an amazing thing.

Second, we know it can be done because it has been done. You've read in the last chapters that billions of people aren't as poor or unhealthy as they used to be, that they live longer, they're going to school more, and they have more freedoms and opportunities. It isn't impossible to make things better, even for billions —it is what the world has been doing again and again since your grandparents were born.

And we have solutions to the challenges we still face. They may cost money or require cooperation, but we know pretty much what to do. The challenges are far from hopeless, they're a call to action.

Third, all that change wasn't done by one person, it was done by people working together — hundreds, millions, and billions of people. To make a global difference we need to cooperate.

That isn't the way you usually hear about how change happens. Just like we can understand and relate to an individual story of tragedy better than we can a story that involves hundreds or thousands or millions of people, we like stories about progress that involve a hero. And there are certainly enough brave, thoughtful, and good people on the planet to call heroes. Think of Neil Armstrong on the moon, Rosa Parks sitting at the front of the bus in Montgomery, or Dr. Dilip Mahalanabis mixing up barrels of water, sugar and salt in a Bangladesh refugee camp to treat hundreds of cases of deadly diarrhea caused by cholera.

But the world doesn't get better because of one person, it gets better because of lots of people working together. Neil Armstrong was only first on the moon because of the rocket scientists, engineers, accountants, managers, and politicians who made sure there was a rocket that flew to the moon in the first place. Rosa Parks was joined by hundreds of others in boycotting a bus system that made black people sit at the back, and that is what forced change. Mahalanabis' solution was the product of a team of researchers and has only saved lives worldwide because so many doctors and nurses and parents now use it. Being part of something bigger than yourself is the way you'll make the world better.

And because it takes a lot of people working together, when you want to make a big change, it is likely to involve government. Jeff Bezos, who owns Amazon, is very, very, rich –indeed, in 2020, he was the world's richest person. But everything he owns is worth about the same as the US government spends in a couple of weeks. There is nothing bigger than a government, and while there is nothing bigger than the harm that governments can do, there is nothing greater than the good they can do, either.

So, if you want to help change the world, you are probably going to have to work with or in a government. It is governments (most places) that educate children. It is governments (most places) who run health care. It is governments that have armies and police forces. It is governments who stop people polluting and who collect the trash. Name the things you want to change, and governments are going to matter. For all you might not like the President, or believe your Congressperson, or know who your mayor is (if you have one), these people really matter when it comes to solving big problems.

Global change is also going to take global cooperation. A lot more of the problems of today are worldwide in scope. They can't be solved without countries working together. Think about the oceans –even if everybody in California and Washington State, Hawaii and Oregon stopped dumping trash in the Pacific, the ocean wouldn't get clean unless Japan, China, Australia, Mexico, and a whole bunch of other countries did the same thing.

But if any generation can manage world-spanning cooperation, it is yours. The 2,720,000,000 people born worldwide between 2001 and 2020 are the healthiest set of children ever. They are the most educated. They are the freest, and they will have more technologies to achieve more things than ever before. This generation will still be human —there will be bullies, liars and cheats, the misguided and malevolent. And too many will live lives of extreme hardship. But it will still be the best prepared of any set of people in the history of the world to tackle the challenges it will face, from climate change to new infectious disease threats. It will be amazing to watch what you accomplish.

Sources

The main sources for the global data in this book are Steven Pinker's *Enlightenment Now and The Better Angels of Our Nature* and the websites ourworldindata.org, humanprogress.org and gapminder.org. A lot of US data comes from the Bureau of Labor Statistics and the Census as well as the St Louis branch of US Federal Reserve's online data collection called FRED. The United Nations collects data on all sorts of things –including births, deaths and marriages. I also used a book I wrote a few years ago called *Getting Better: Why Global Development is Succeeding,* which discusses global development progress. The examples of activism by young people draw heavily on Vicky Johnson, Tessa Lewin, and Mariah Cannon "Learning from a Living Archive: Rejuvenating Child and Youth Rights and Participation" Rejuvenate Working Paper 1, December 2020.

In the introduction, I used Pew research center data on attitudes and The World Happiness Report. The statistic on how many people the average person knows comes from a New York Times article "The Average American Knows How Many People?" (2/18/2013).

For the health chapter, data on US drug prescriptions from Fuentes et al. (2018) Comprehension of Top 200 Prescribed Drugs in the US as a Resource for Pharmacy Teaching, Training and Practice. The website Historyofvaccines.org and Centers for Disease Control website on illness in the United States. The details of the Disney measles outbreak come from the CDC's Morbidity and Mortality Weekly Report 64(06) 153-154.

For the money chapter, data on pet spending comes from APPA Pet Industry Market Size & Ownership Statistics and Pet Food Processing State of the US pet food and treat industry reports. Data on Tanzanian poverty at the US ($17) poverty line is from the World Bank's povcalnet. The description of the Kaburas is from Gapminder/Dollar Street.

For the home chapter, Sclatter's possessions are recorded in Furnishings of medieval English peasant houses: investment, consumption and life style, a mimeo by Christopher Dyer of the University of Leicester.

For the school chapter, Dutch literacy rate data is from Akçomak, İ. S., Webbink, D., & Ter Weel, B. (2015). Why did the Netherlands develop so early? The legacy of the brethren of the common life. *The Economic Journal, 126*(593), 821-860. Data on enrollments in Malala's district are from Sumbal Naveed *The importance of educating girls in the Newly Merged Districts of Khyber Pakhtunkhwa, Pakistan* Brookings, 2018.

For the work and leisure chapter, I use the report No Vacation Nation, Revised, by Adewale Maye for the Center for Economic and Policy Research.

For the crime and violence chapter, Neta Crawford at Brown University tracks the casualties of recent wars, and Peter Bergen wrote about The golden age of terrorism for CNN.com.

For the freedom chapter, Gallup provides on attitudes in the US and the World Bank's Women

Business and the Law database includes data on women's legal rights. Information on global Black Lives Matter protests came from the website https://www.creosotemaps.com/blm2020/

For the democracy chapter, data on the number of people voting in 1790 come from Wikipedia (the 1790 census reports free white males over the age of 16 made up 20 percent of the population, I assume about half of that population had the right to vote). the Washington quote is from his letter to the Hebrew Congregation in Newport, Rhode Island in 1790. The data on more recent voting by race is from the United State Elections Project: http://www.electproject.org/home/voter-turnout/demographics. The data on worldwide attitudes towards democracy comes from the World Values Survey. The fact that most members of Congress are millionaires is from OpenSecrets.org.

For the environment chapter, US air pollution data is from Zhang, Y., West, J. J., Mathur, R., Xing, J., Hogrefe, C., Roselle, S. J., Bash, J. O., Pleim, J. E., Gan, C.-M., and Wong, D. C.: Long-term trends in the ambient $PM_{2.5}$- and O_3-related mortality burdens in the United States under emission reductions from 1990 to 2010, Atmos. Chem. Phys., 18, 15003–15016. The risk of dying in a climate-related natural disaster is from Formetta, G., & Feyen, L. (2019). Empirical evidence of declining global vulnerability to climate-related hazards. *Global Environmental Change, 57,* 101920. The data on extinctions ins from Sagoff, M. "Welcome to the Narcisscine" *The Breakthrough* June 26, 2018.

For the happiness chapter I use my paper "Were People in the Past Poor or Miserable," published in the journal *Kyklos.* The chart data on US happiness comes from the US General Social Survey. The information on suicide in the US comes from the Society for the Prevention of Teen Suicide website. The data on depression comes from the National Institute of Mental Health.

For the future chapter, evidence on attitudes about climate and the future come from the Pew report *Looking to the Future, Public Sees an America in Decline on Many Fronts.* The data on long term economic and population growth is from David Roodman's paper *Superexponential.*

Acknowledgements

Thanks to Sophie Engel, Maya Donnelly-Cohen, Alex Kenny, Sofia Guyer, Mathilda DeCosse, Julia Kenny, Ella Maruszewski, Emily Fleming, Julia Horvath, Eva Doherty, Anthony Kenny, Jill Paton Walsh, James Morris, and Stephanie Morris for insightful (and sometimes delightful) comments and suggestions that led to considerable additions and changes to the text.

Made in the USA
Columbia, SC
15 September 2022

67345362R00109